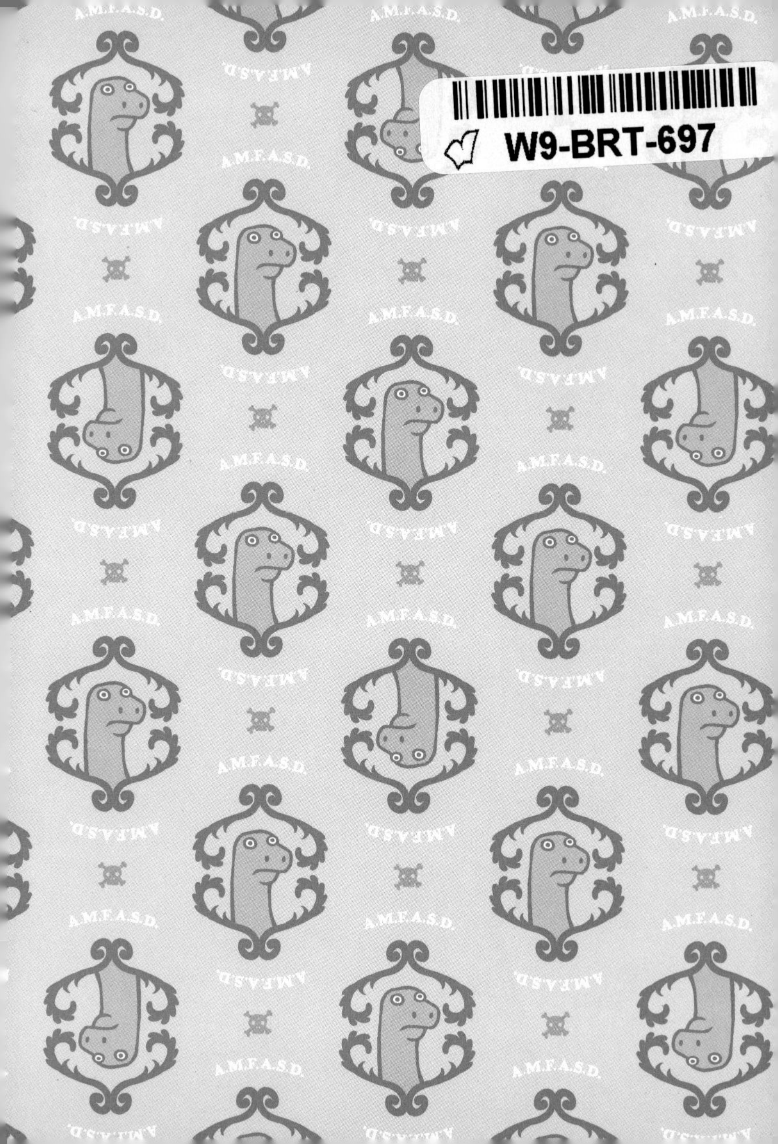
A.M.F.A.S.D.

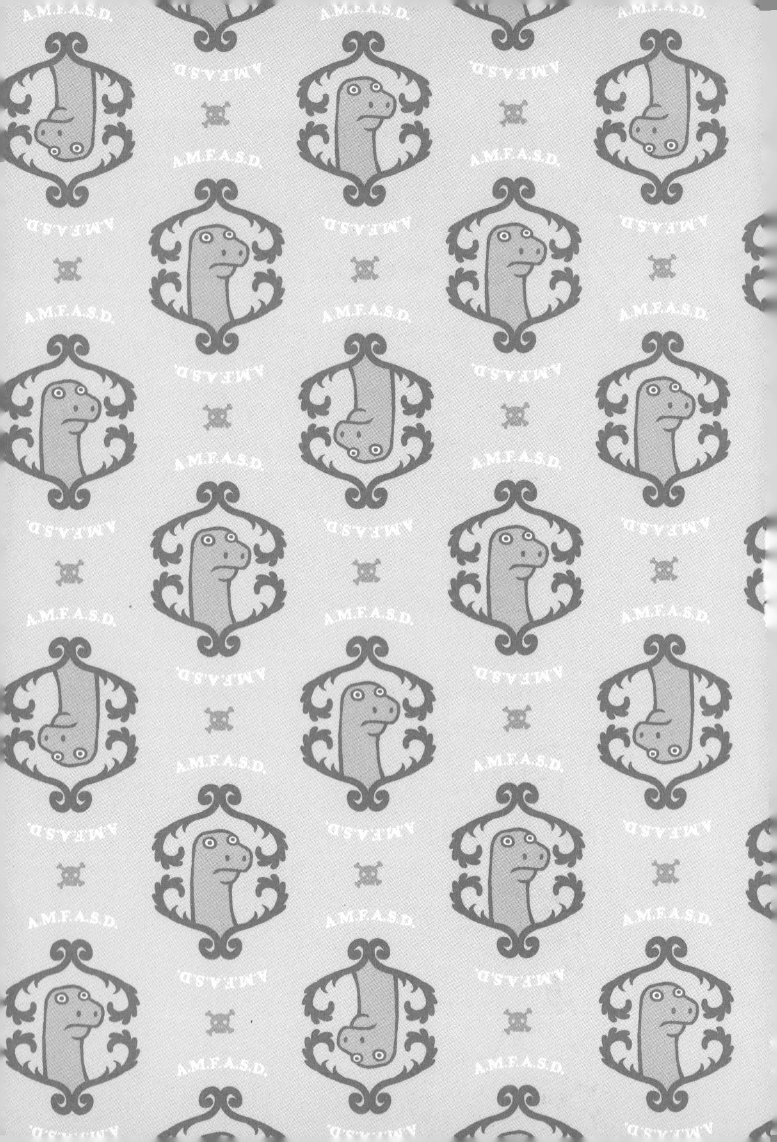
A.M.F.A.S.D.

All my friends are *still* dead.

Text copyright © 2012 by Avery Monsen and Jory John.
Illustrations copyright © 2012 by Avery Monsen.

Library of Congress Cataloging-in-Publication Data

Monsen, Avery.
  All my friends are still dead / Avery Monsen and Jory John.
     p. cm.
  ISBN 978-1-4521-0696-0
1. Death—Humor. 2. American wit and humor, Pictorial. I. John, Jory.
II. Title.

  NC1429.M717A4 2012
  741.5'6973—dc23

                              2011038955

Manufactured in China

Designed by Avery Monsen

10 9 8 7 6 5 4 3

Chronicle Books LLC
680 Second Street
San Francisco, California 94107
www.chroniclebooks.com

All my friends are *still* dead.

Avery Monsen & Jory John

CHRONICLE BOOKS

SAN FRANCISCO

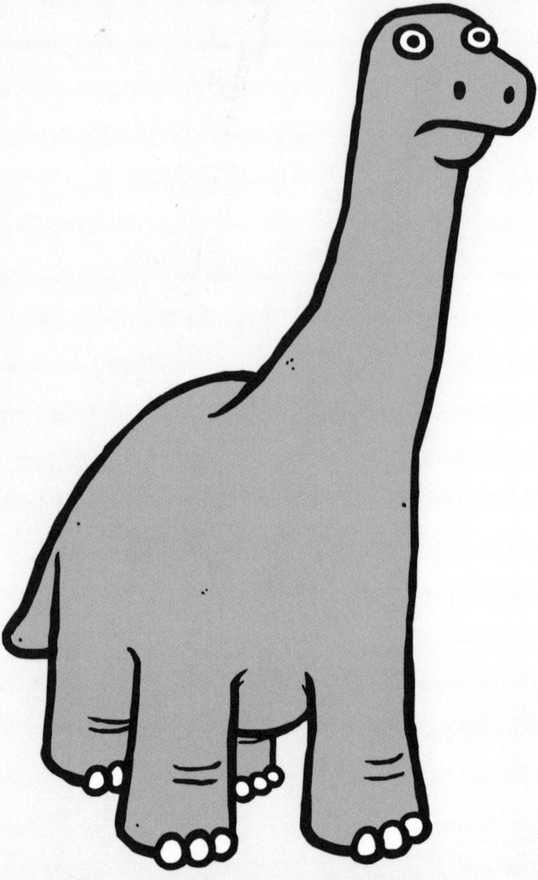

All my friends are still dead.

All *my* friends are still dead.

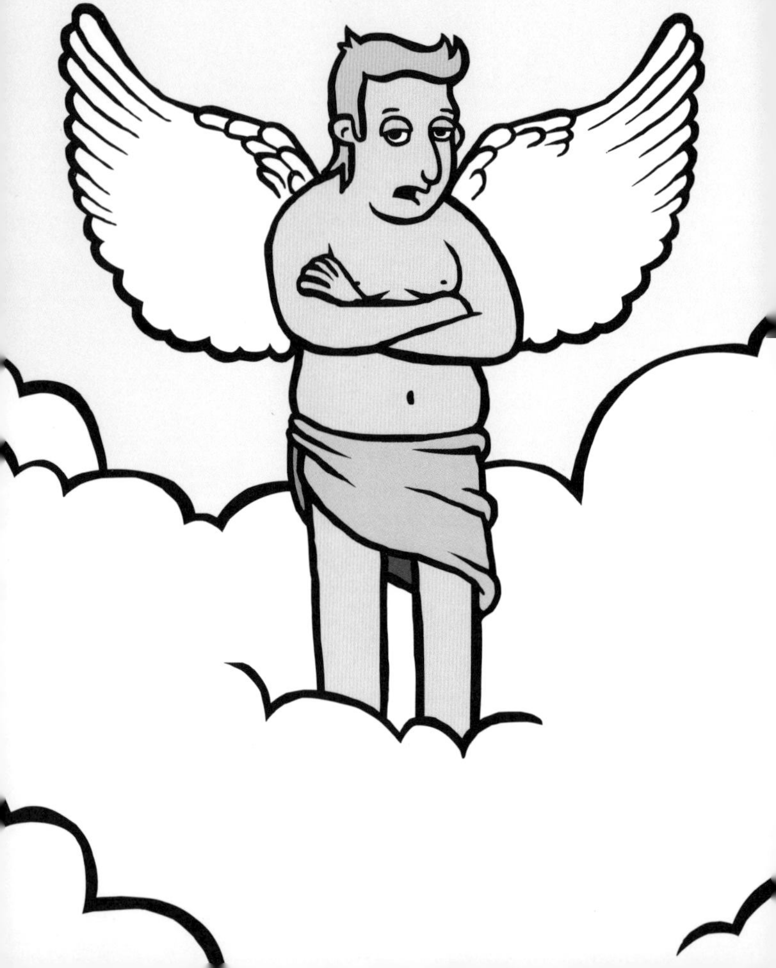

All my
friends are
still alive.

Jerks.

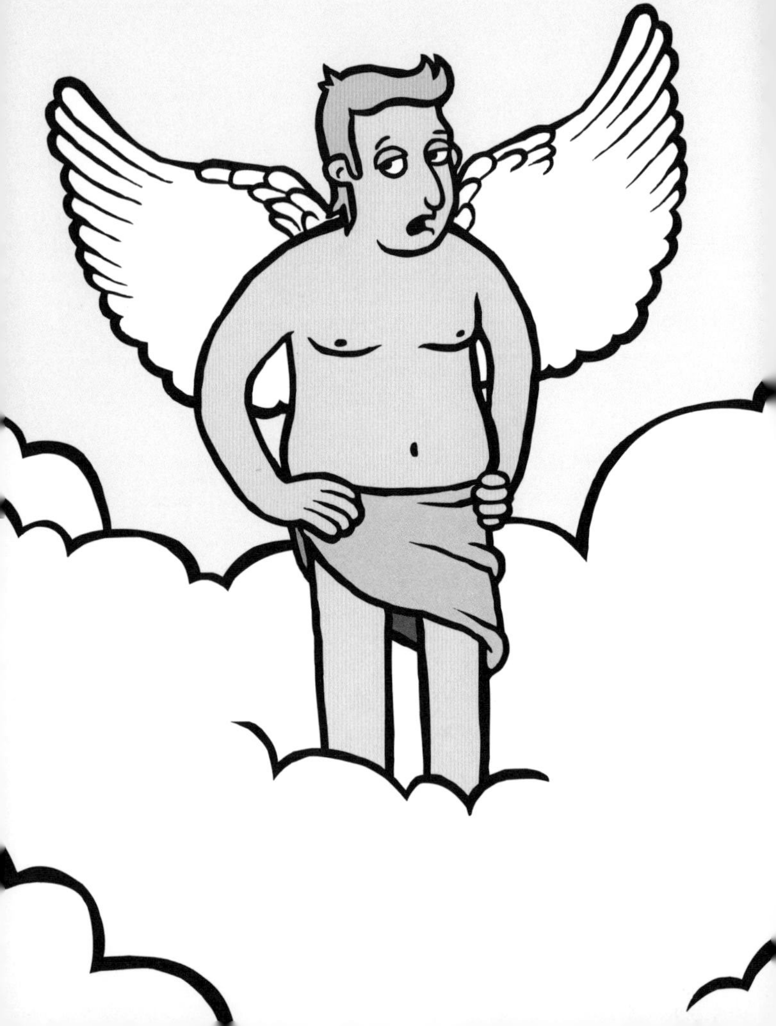

It's *super* boring up here.

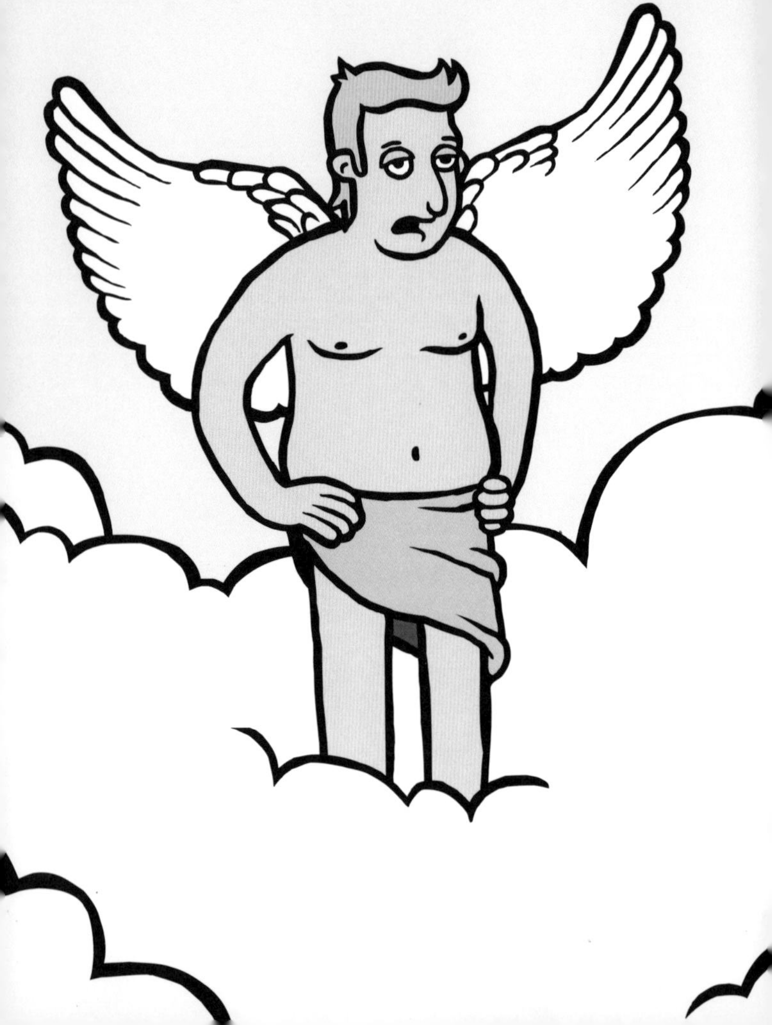

I guess I'm going to go watch some living people showering.

All my
friends
are bacon.

Honestly, we think of him as more of an acquaintance.

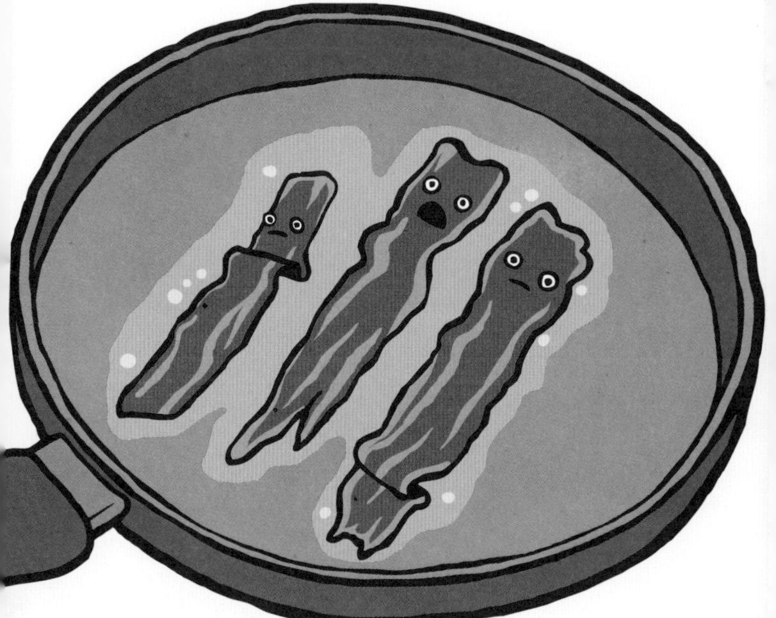

Dangit.

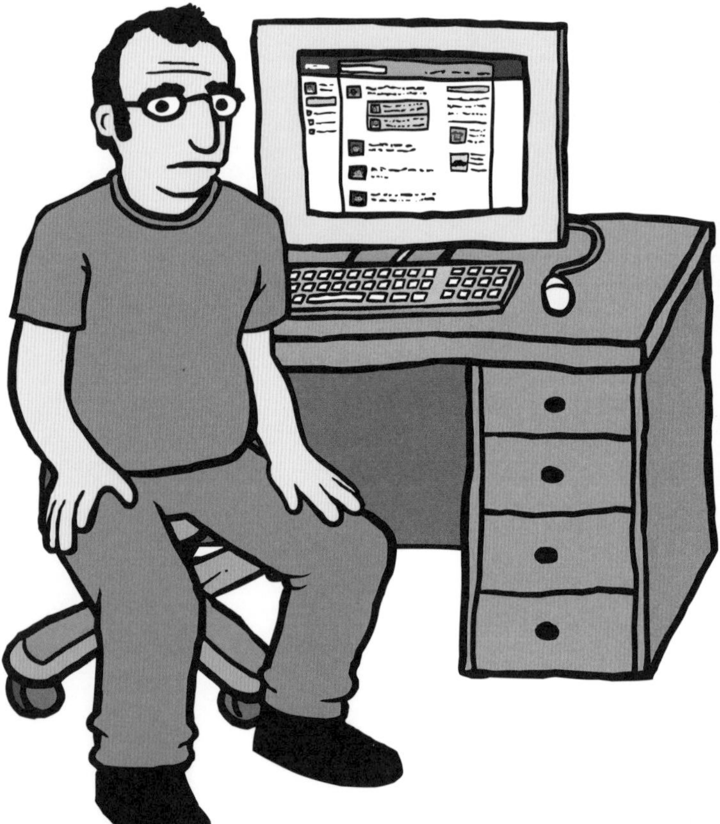

Most of my friends defriended me.

I probably shouldn't have posted all those poems.

I was not
programmed
to understand
the concept
of friendship.

And yet there
is an emptiness
inside me that
I cannot explain.

Let me try.

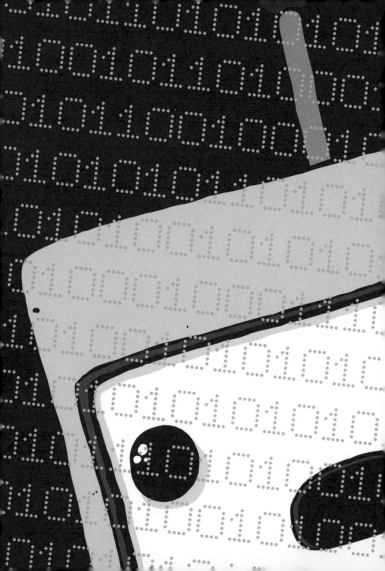

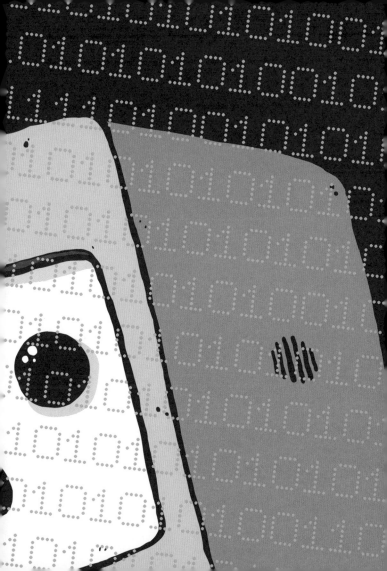

Never-ending solitude.

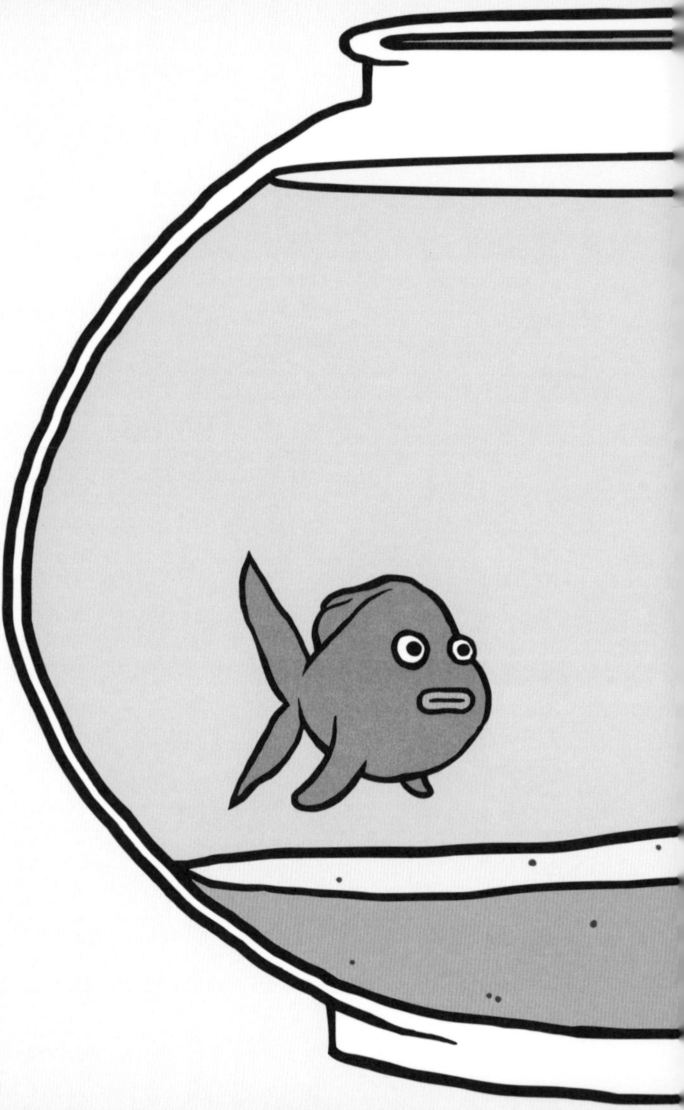

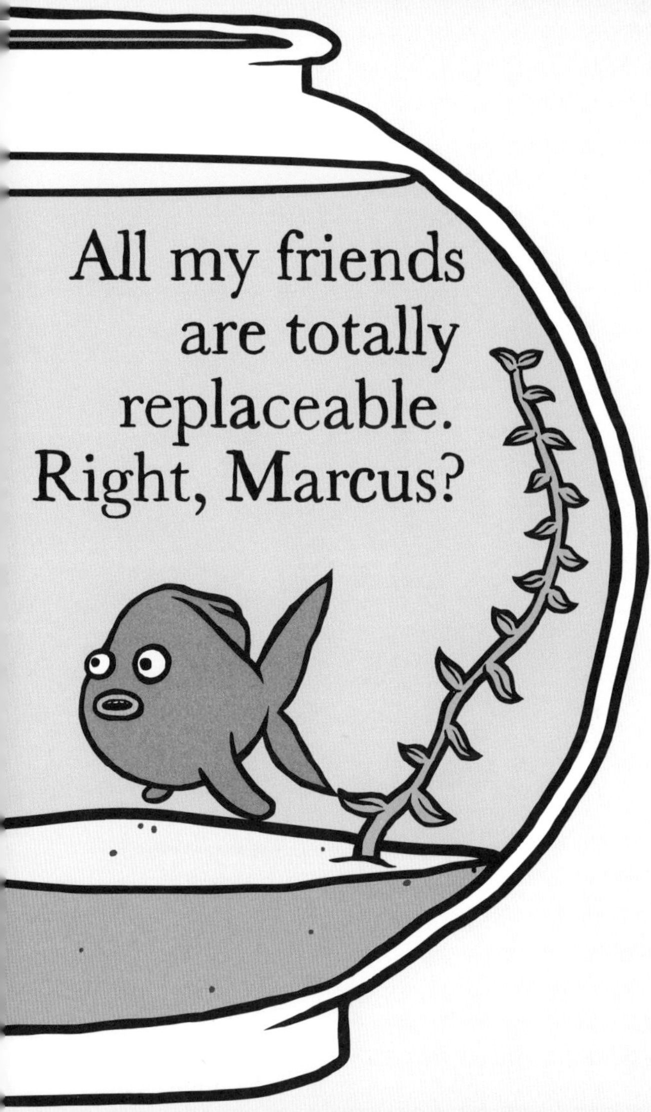
All my friends are totally replaceable. Right, Marcus?

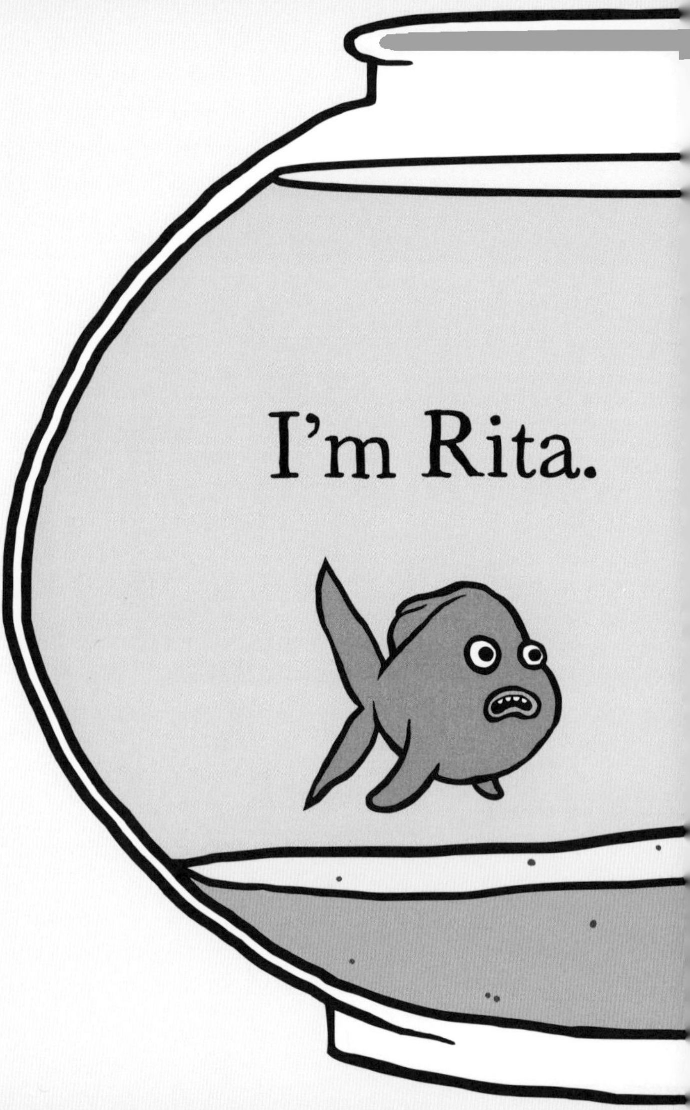

I’m Rita.

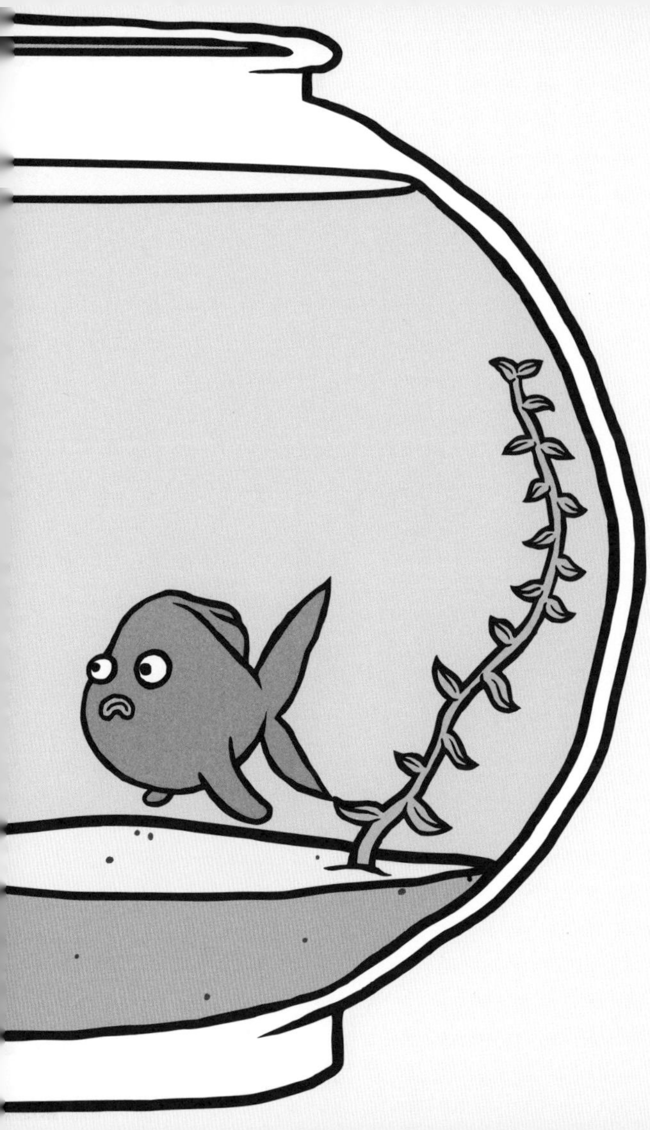

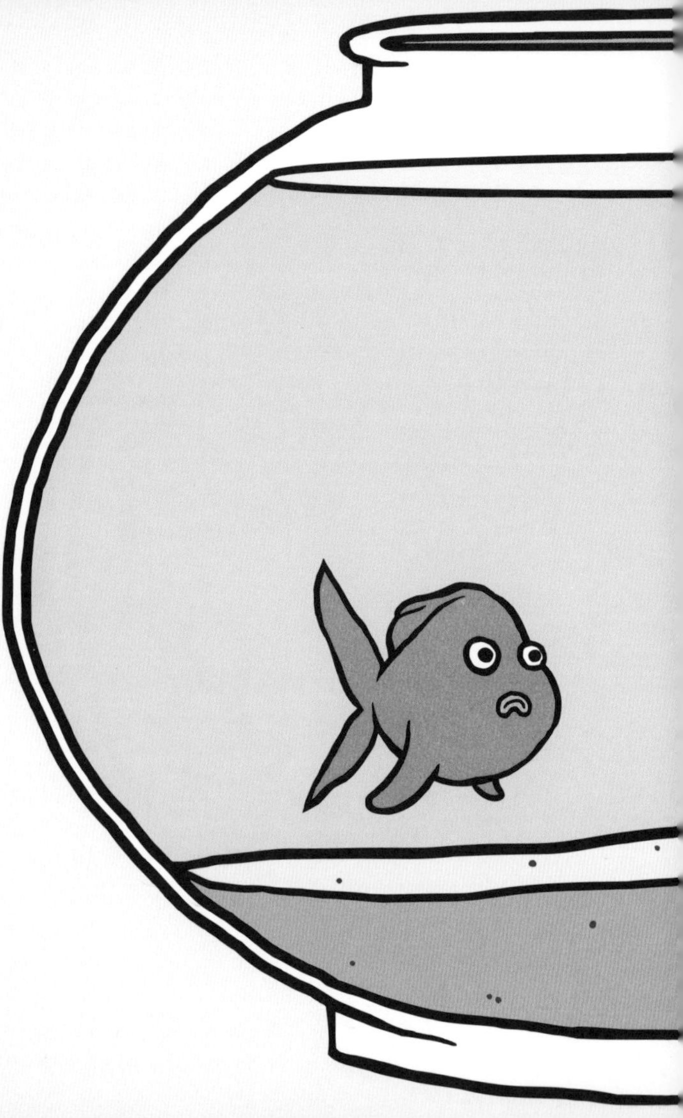

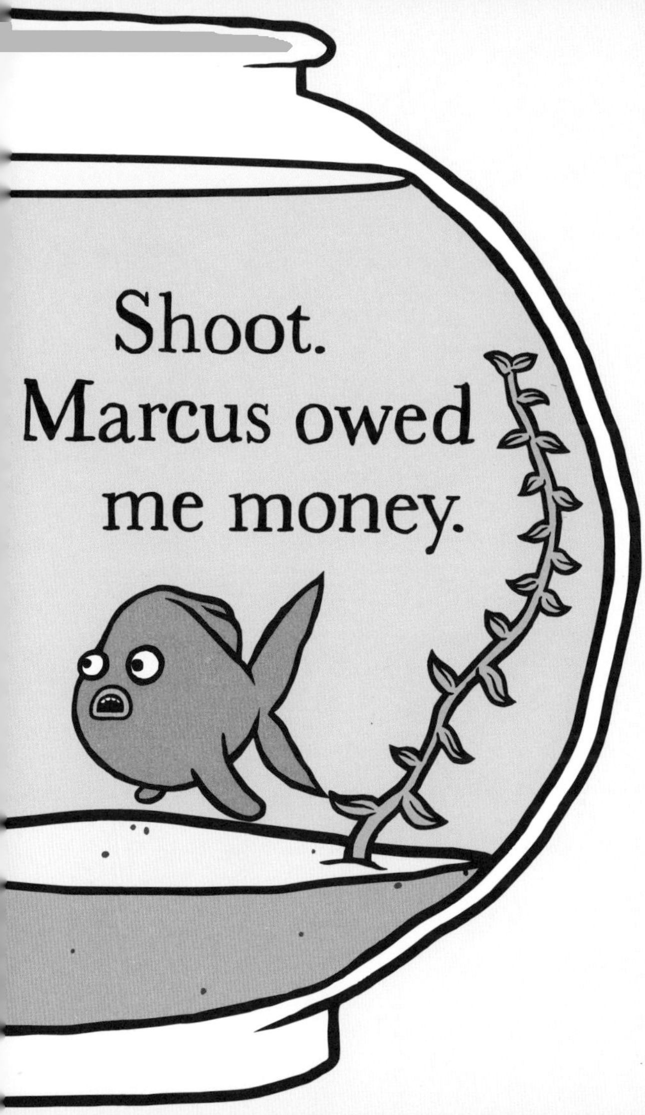

Shoot.
Marcus owed
me money.

All my friends are losers.

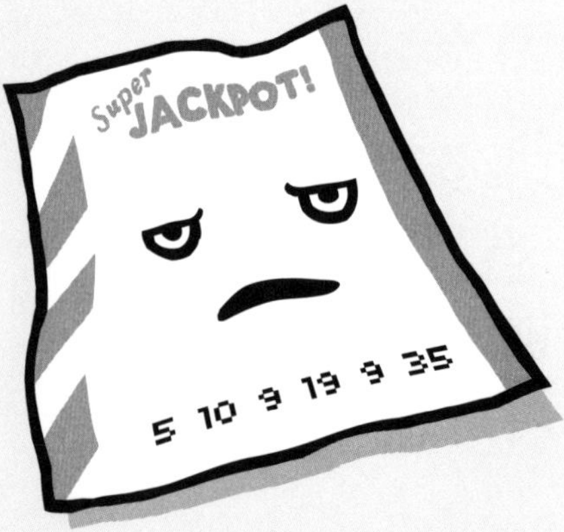
Super JACKPOT!
5 10 9 19 9 35

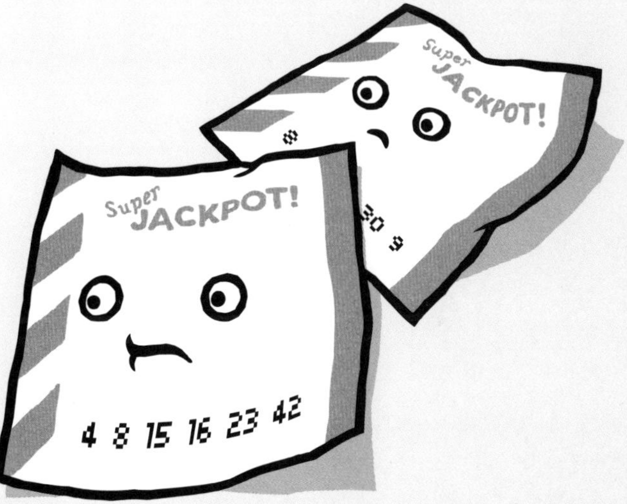
Super JACKPOT!
Super JACKPOT!
4 8 15 16 23 42

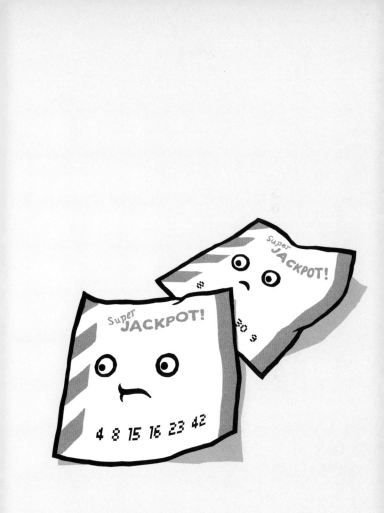

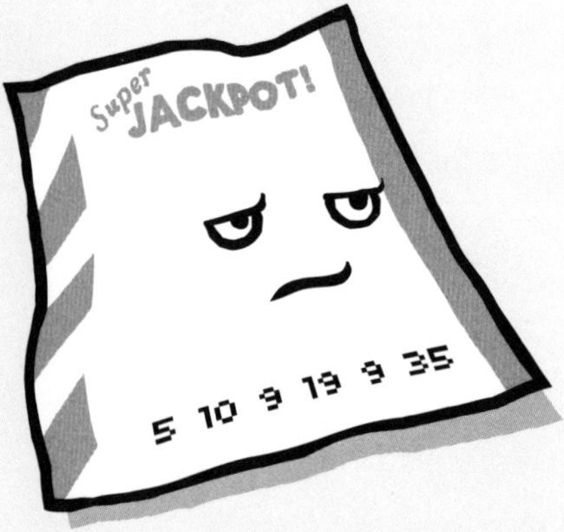
Super
JACKPOT!
5 10 9 19 9 35

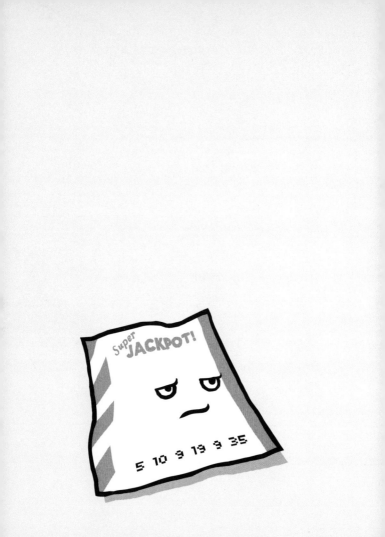

We were just a few numbers off, Jeremy.

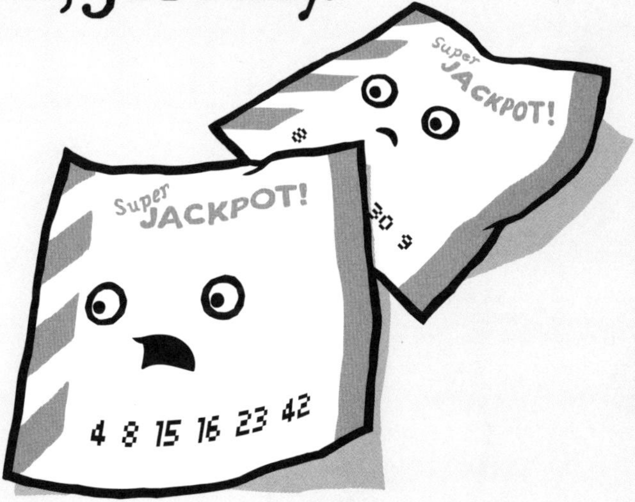

That's what losers say, Rick.

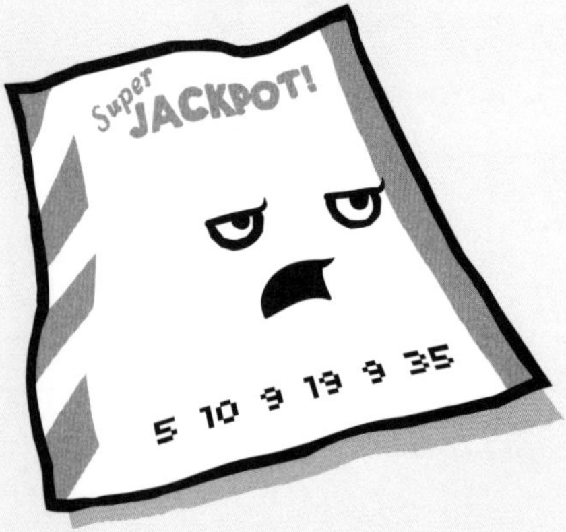
Super JACKPOT!
5 10 9 19 9 35

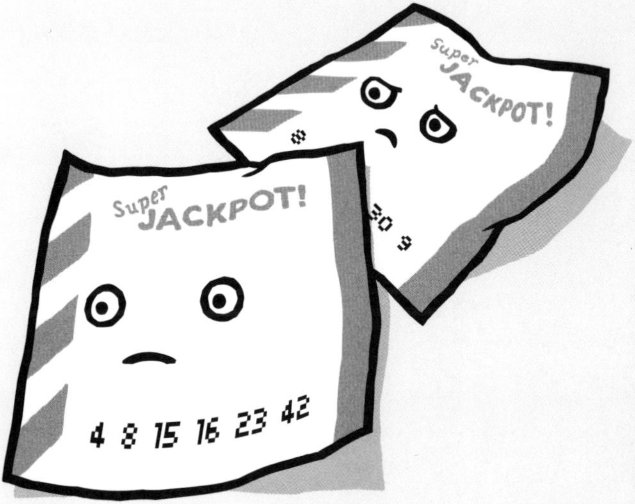
Super JACKPOT!
Super JACKPOT!
4 8 15 16 23 42

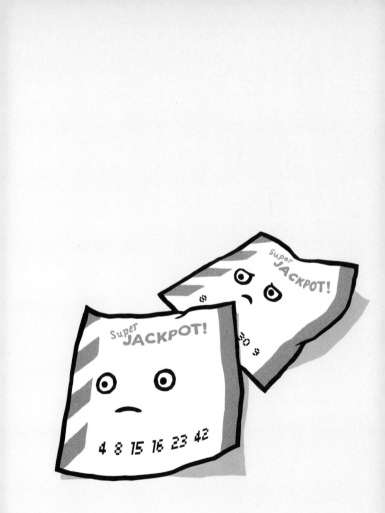

My friends always
die at the absolute
worst times.

All my friends
are garbage.

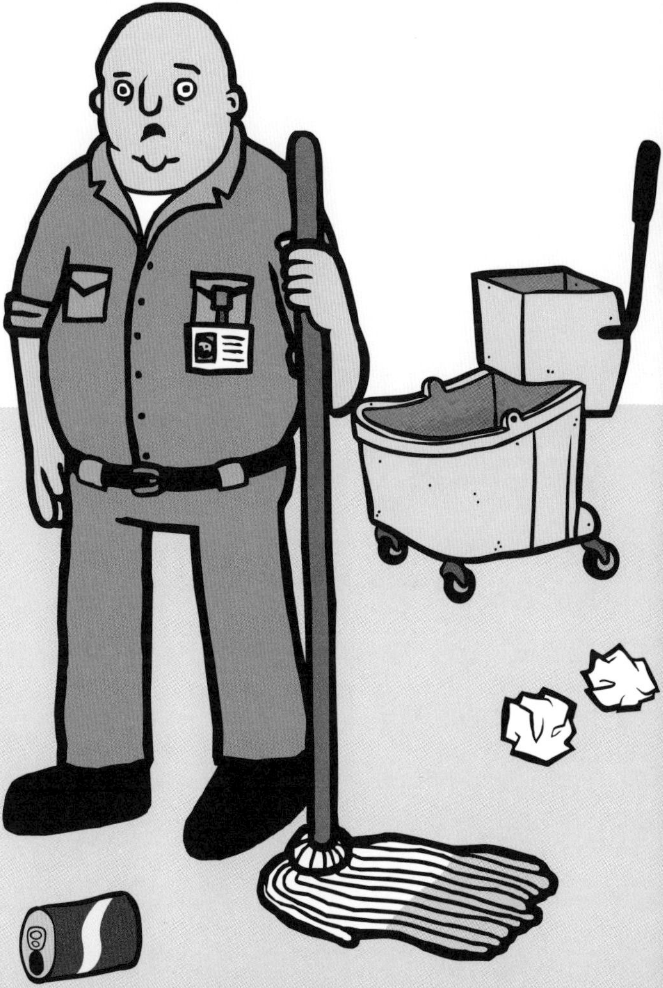

Don't tell nobody, but one time I dressed up a trashcan as a lady.

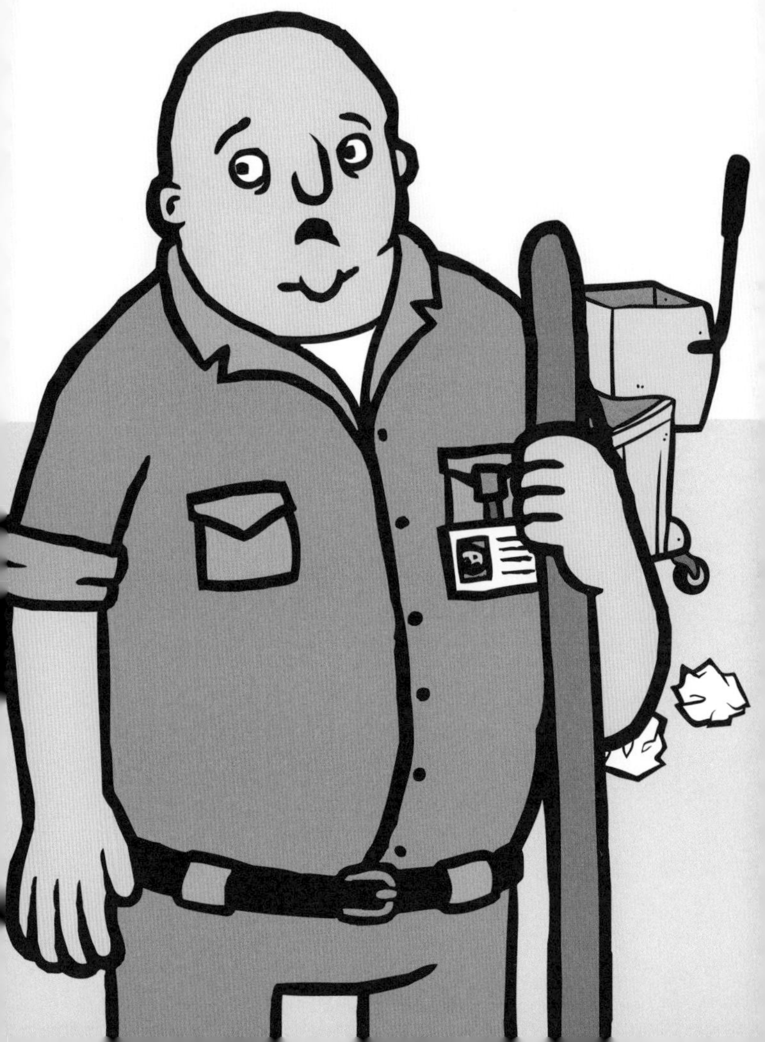

It didn't work out.

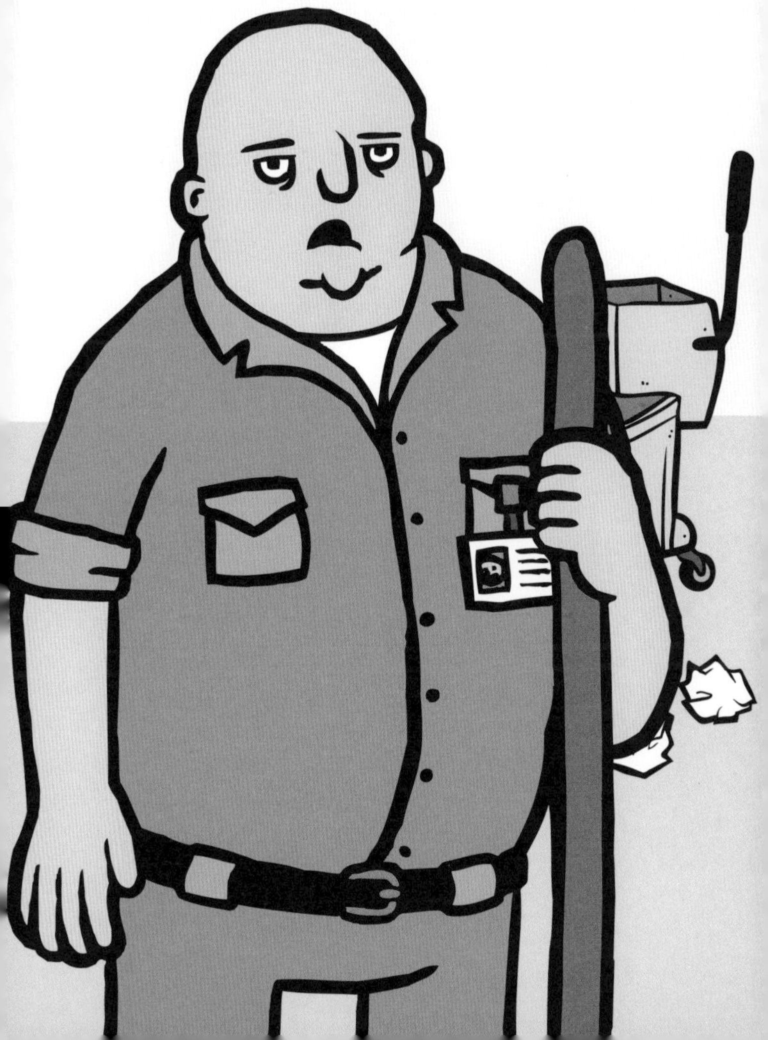

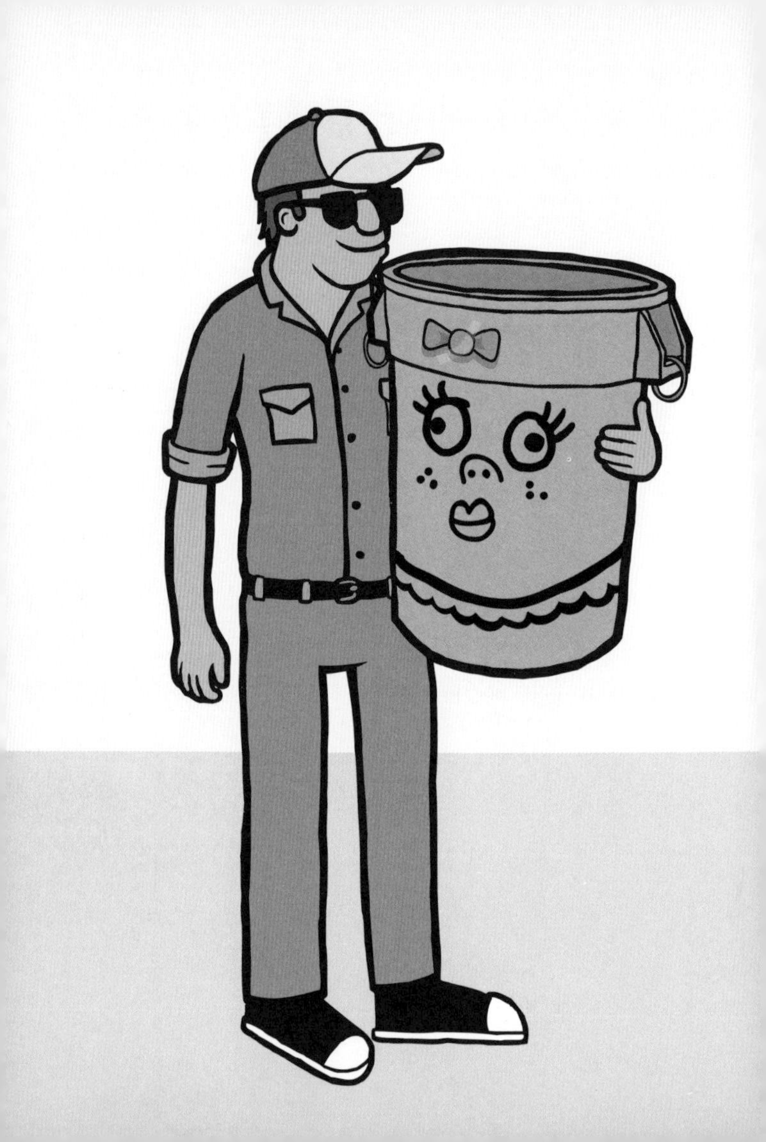

You better treat her right, Joey C.

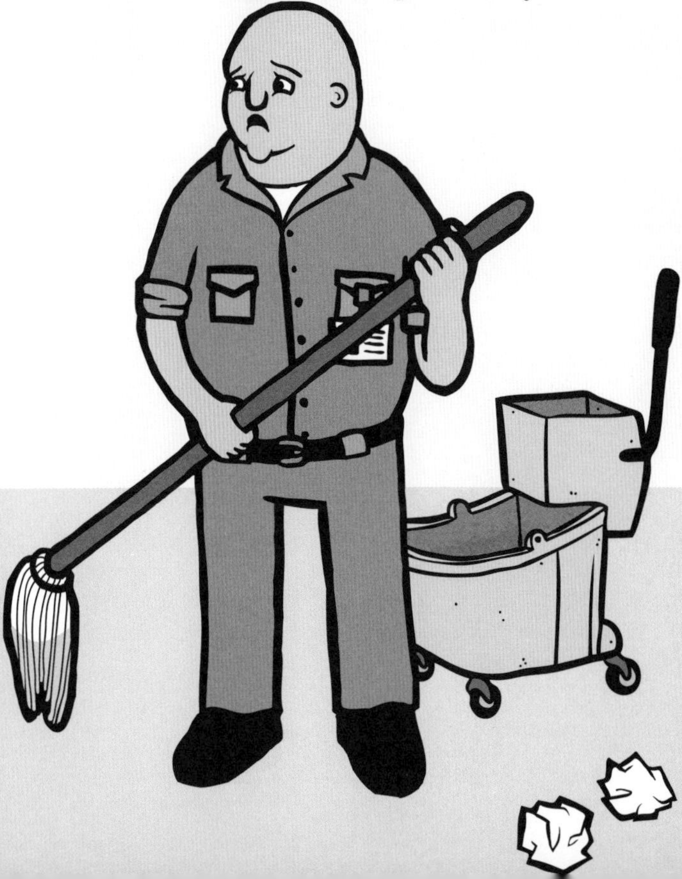

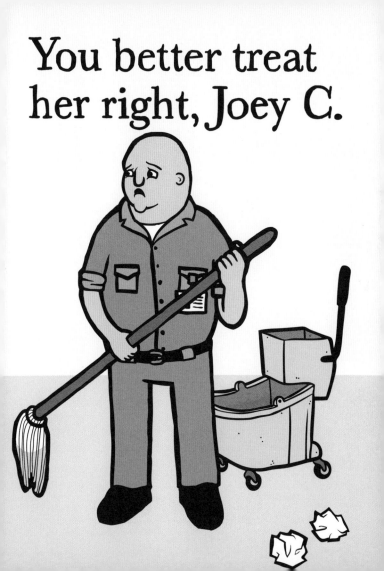

All my friends
will eat all your
dead friends.
It's just what
we do.

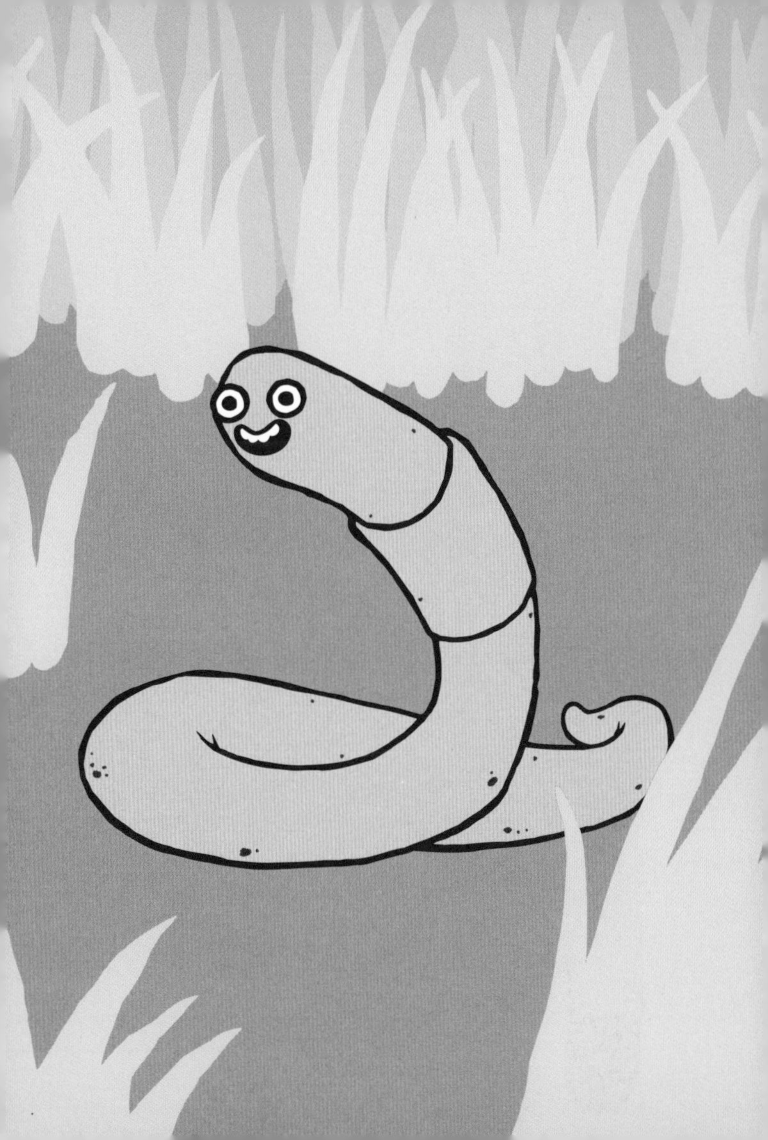

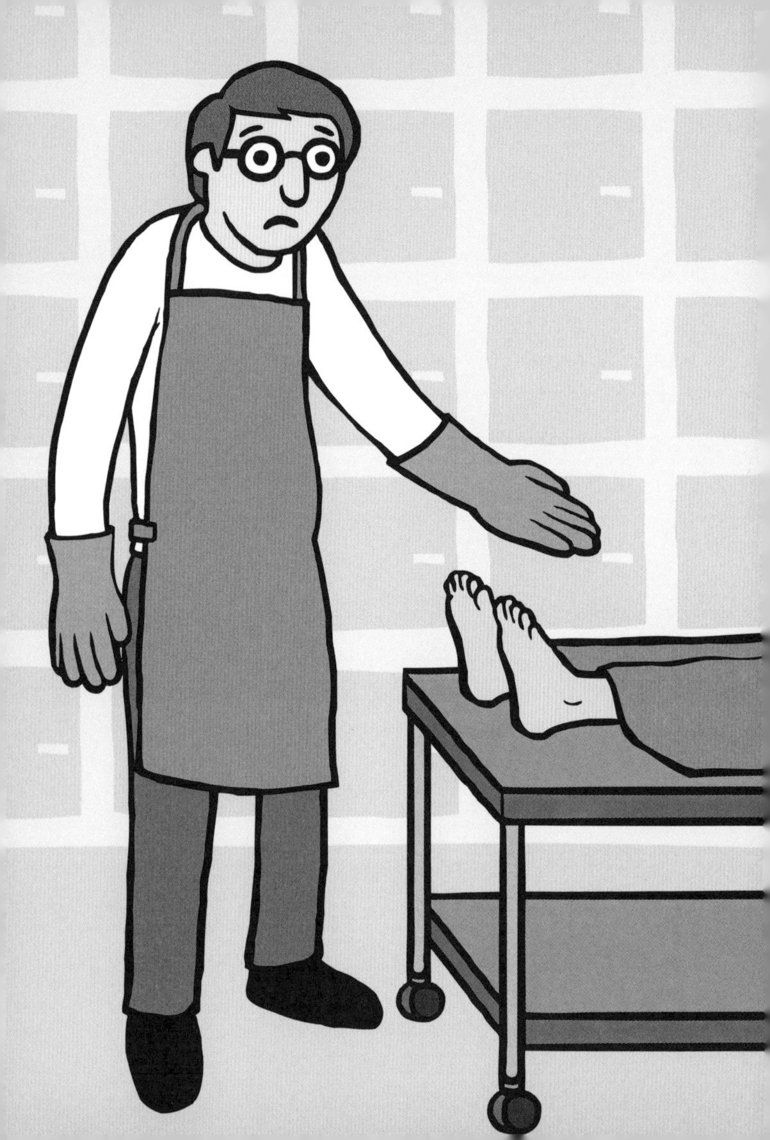

I'm around dead people all the time and I think it's starting to negatively affect my personal life.

God, you're beautiful. You look *exactly* like this one corpse I know.

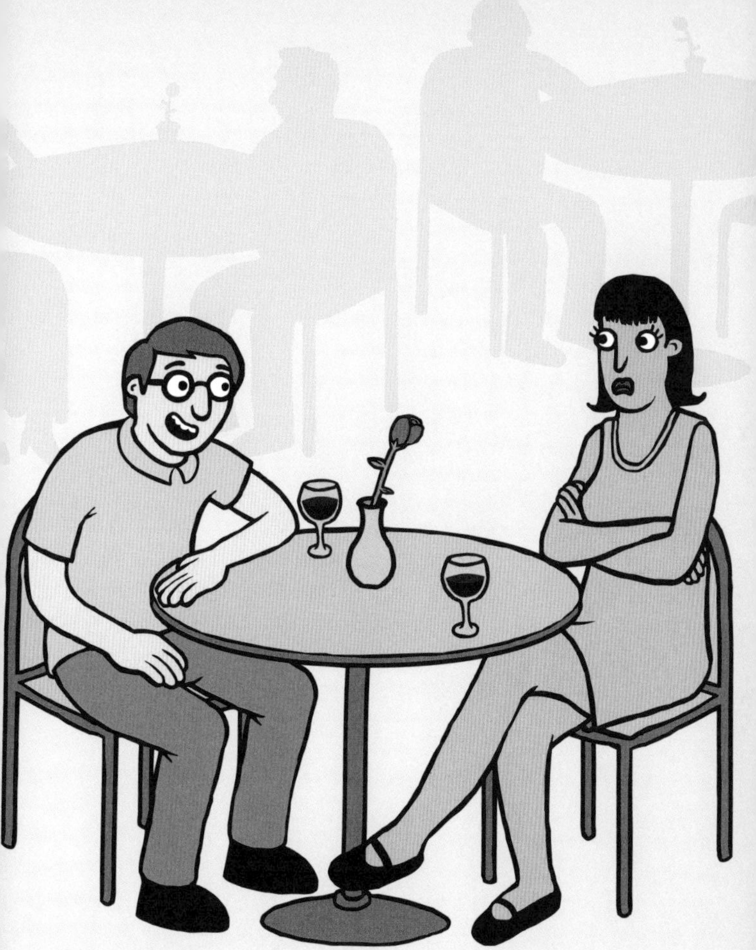

Dangit.

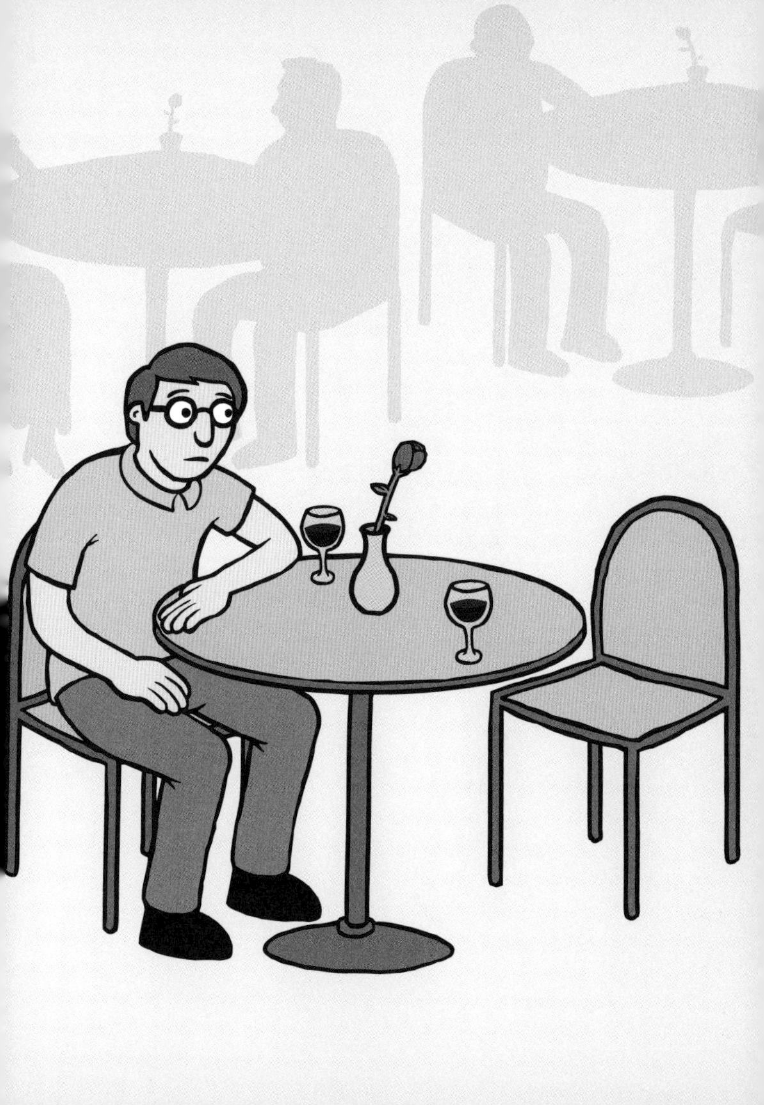

All my
friends
are total
disasters.

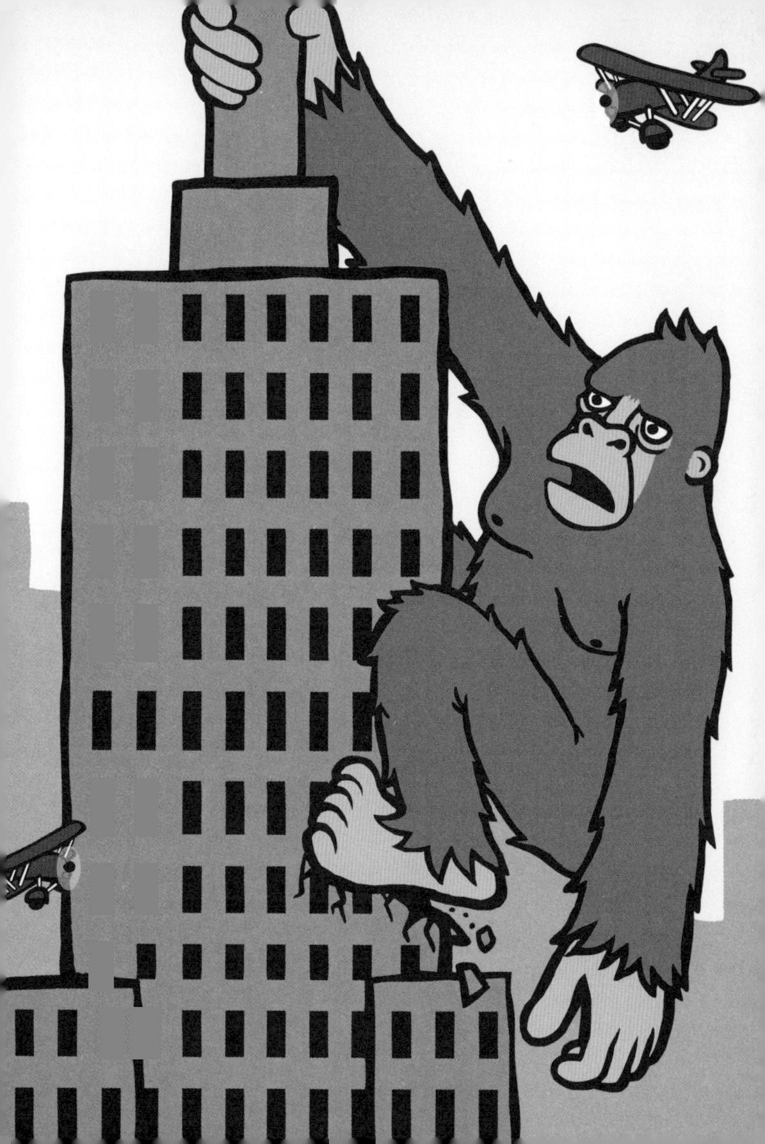

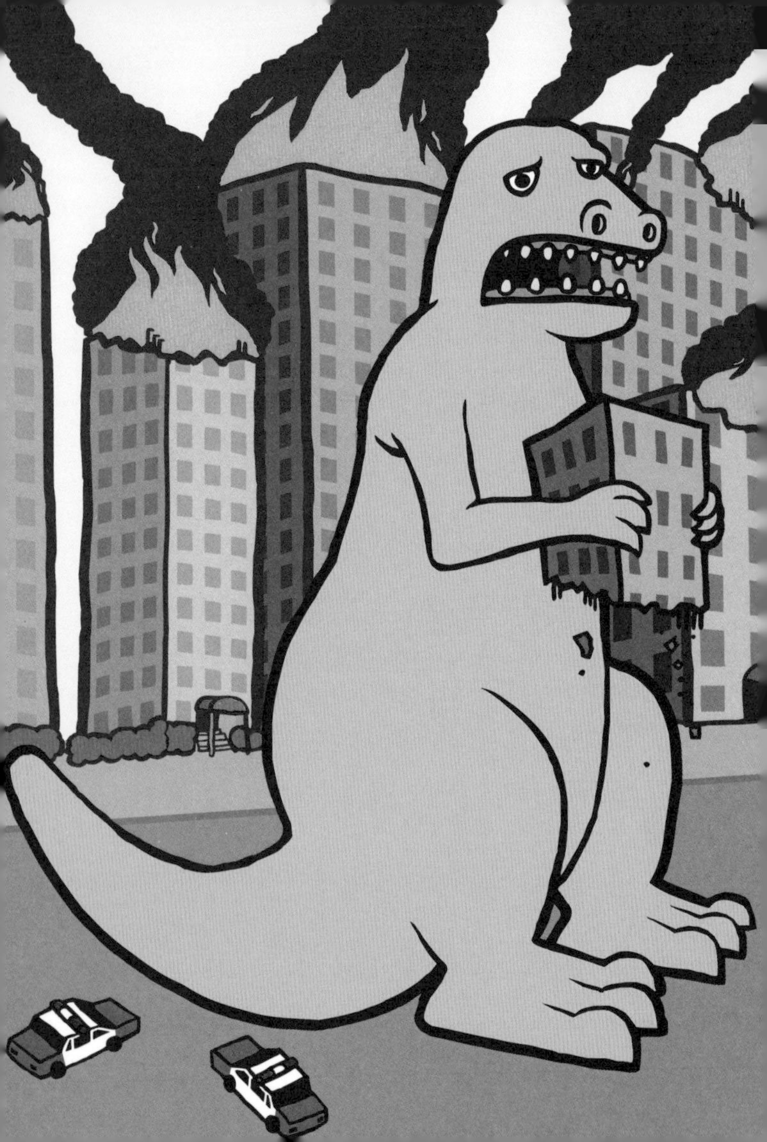

I think I smash buildings because my father was distant.

All my friends are suckers.

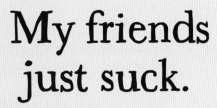

My friends
just suck.

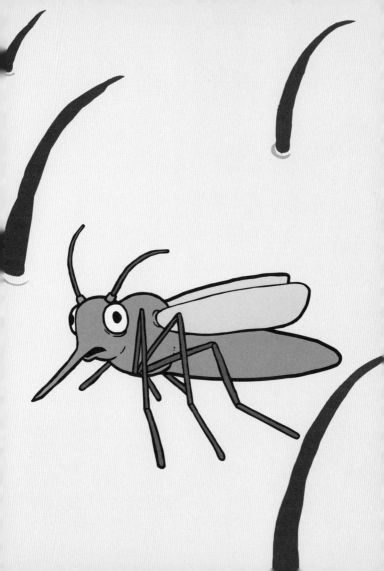

Hello, All-In-One Printer/Scanner. Will you be my friend?

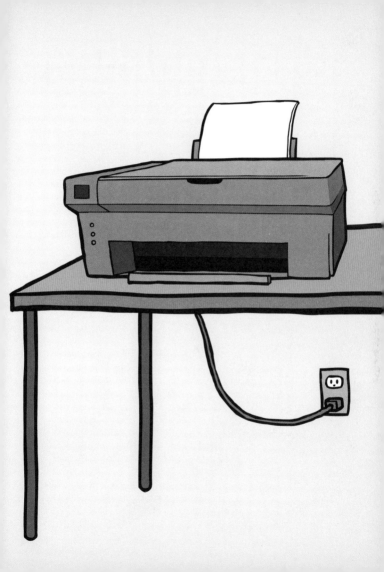

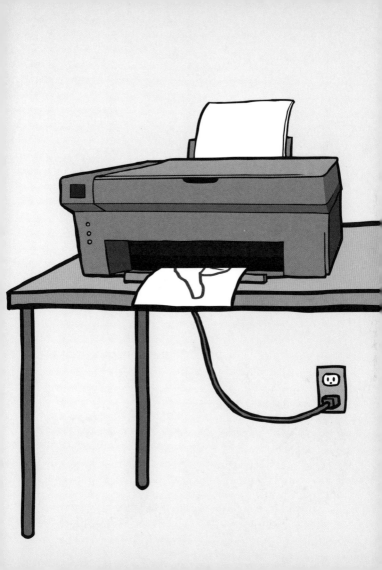

Eternal isolation.

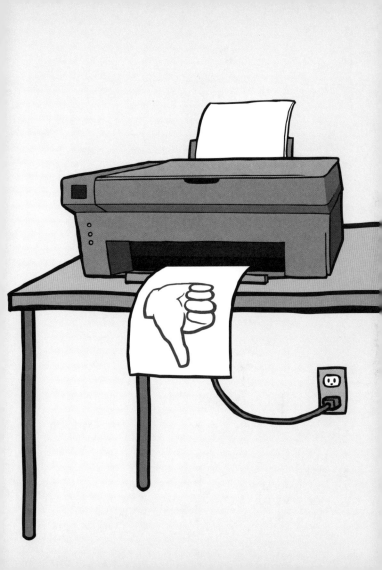

All my friends
are glue.

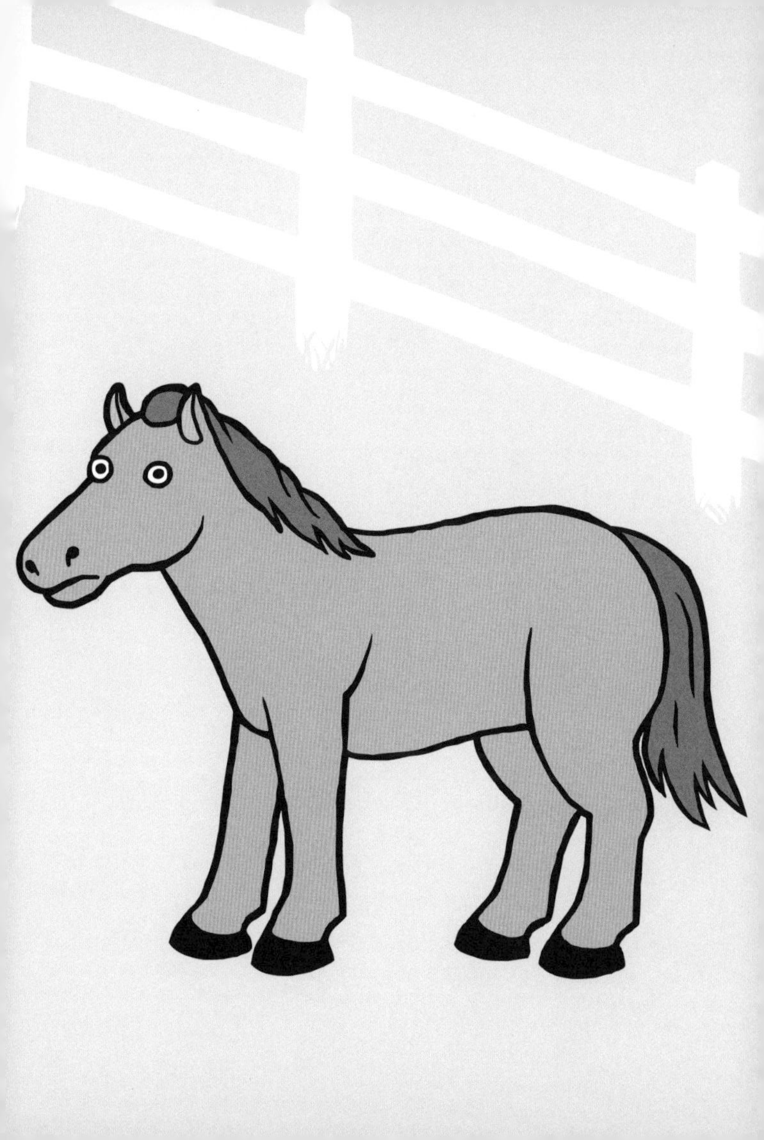

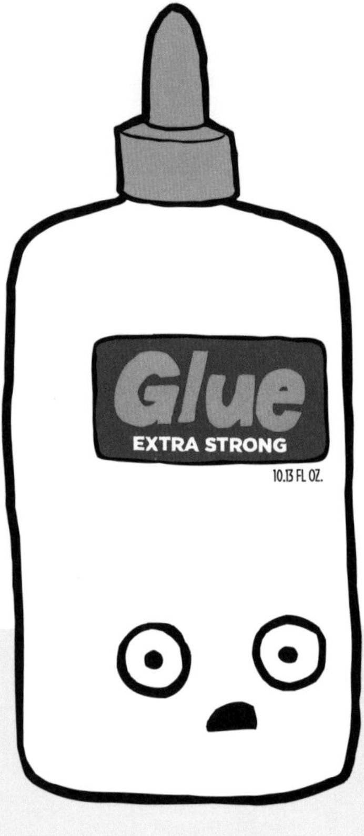
Glue
EXTRA STRONG
10.13 FL OZ.

I won the Kentucky Derby three times.

All my friends
have really
changed.

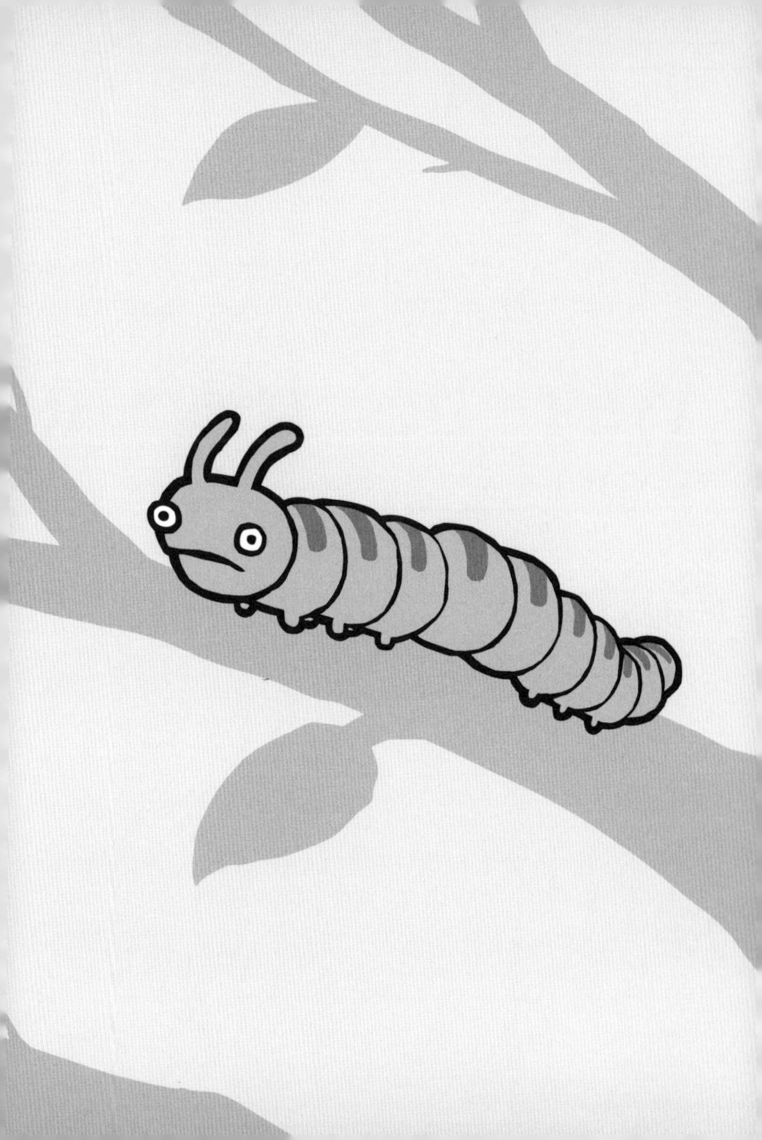

We're best friends!

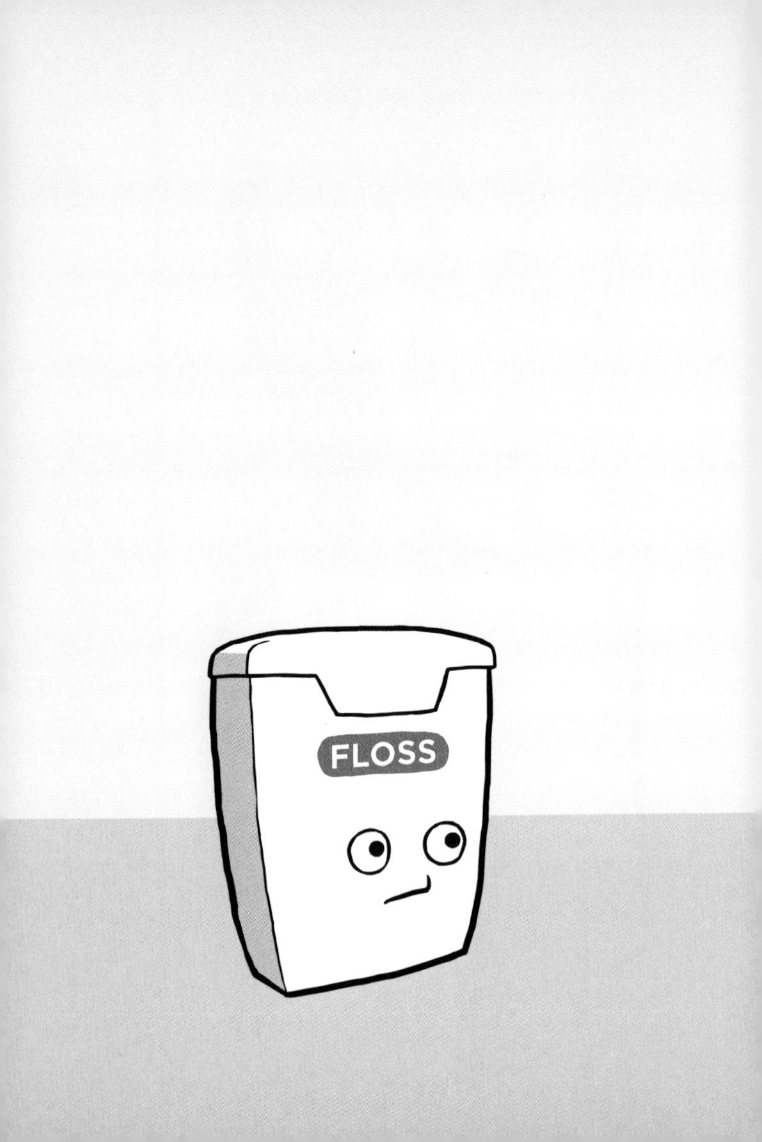
FLOSS

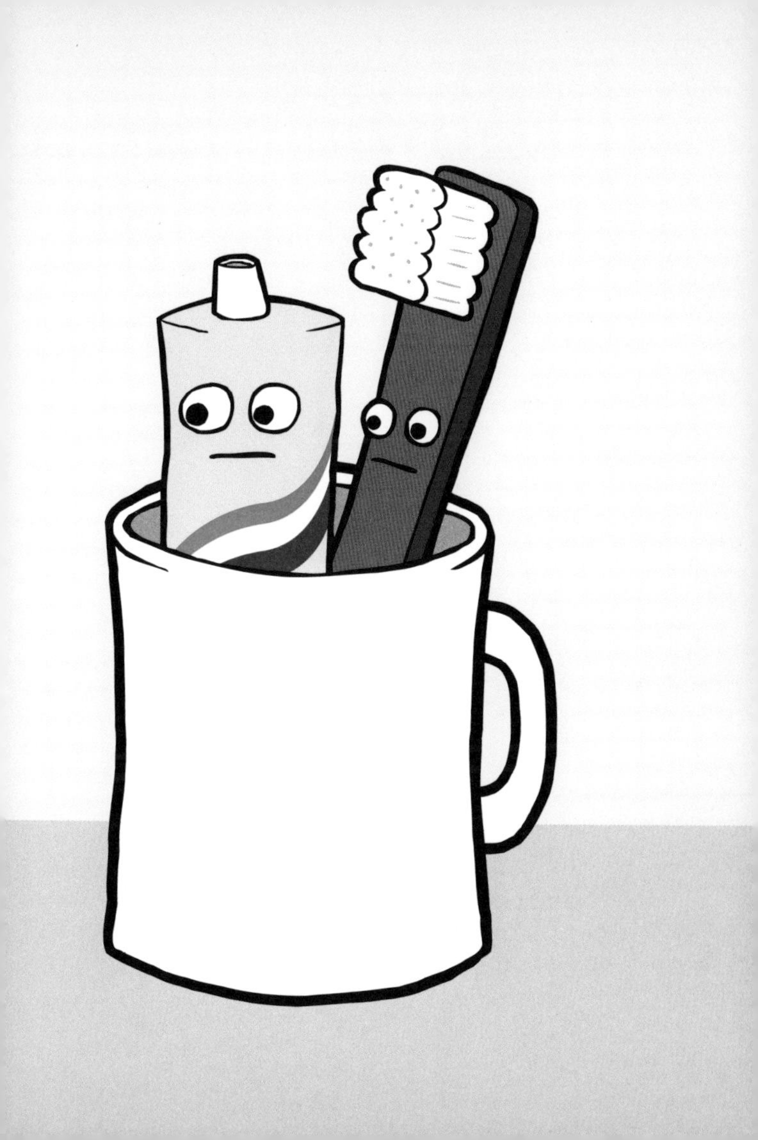

I know it's not intentional, but sometimes you guys really hurt my feelings.

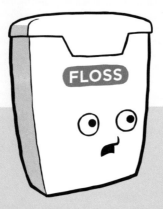

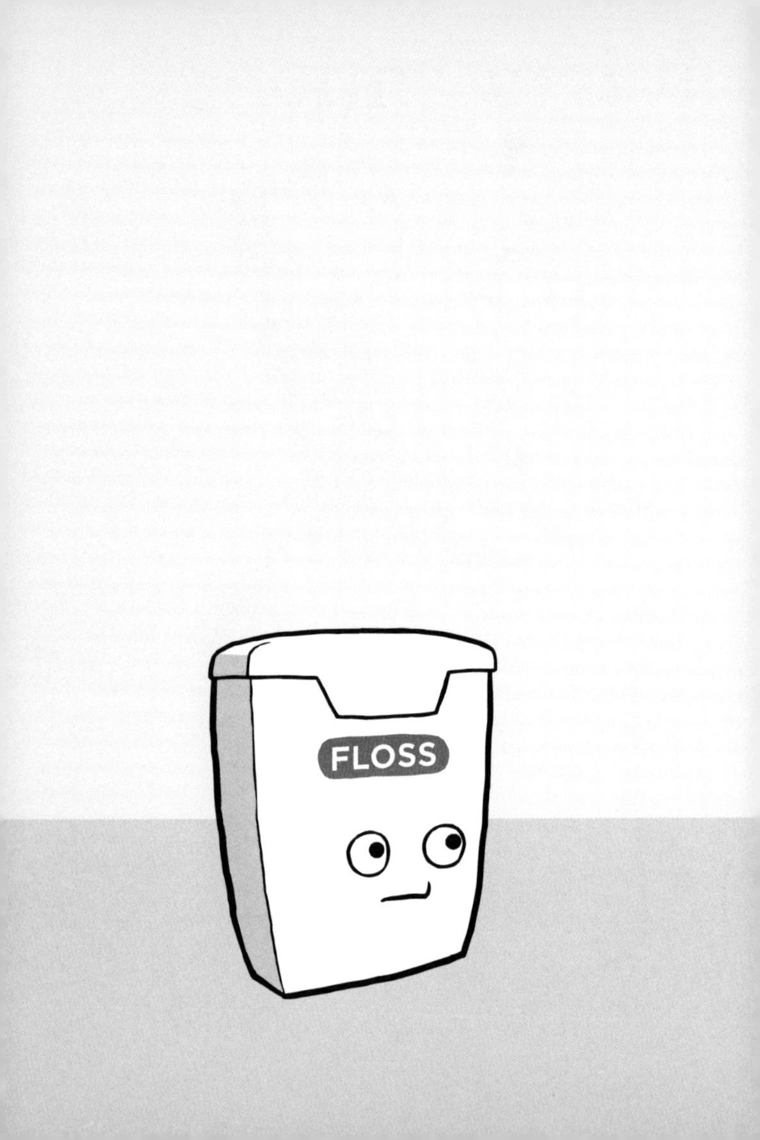
FLOSS

It *is* intentional!

Wow. That was only the second time I've kissed a living person!

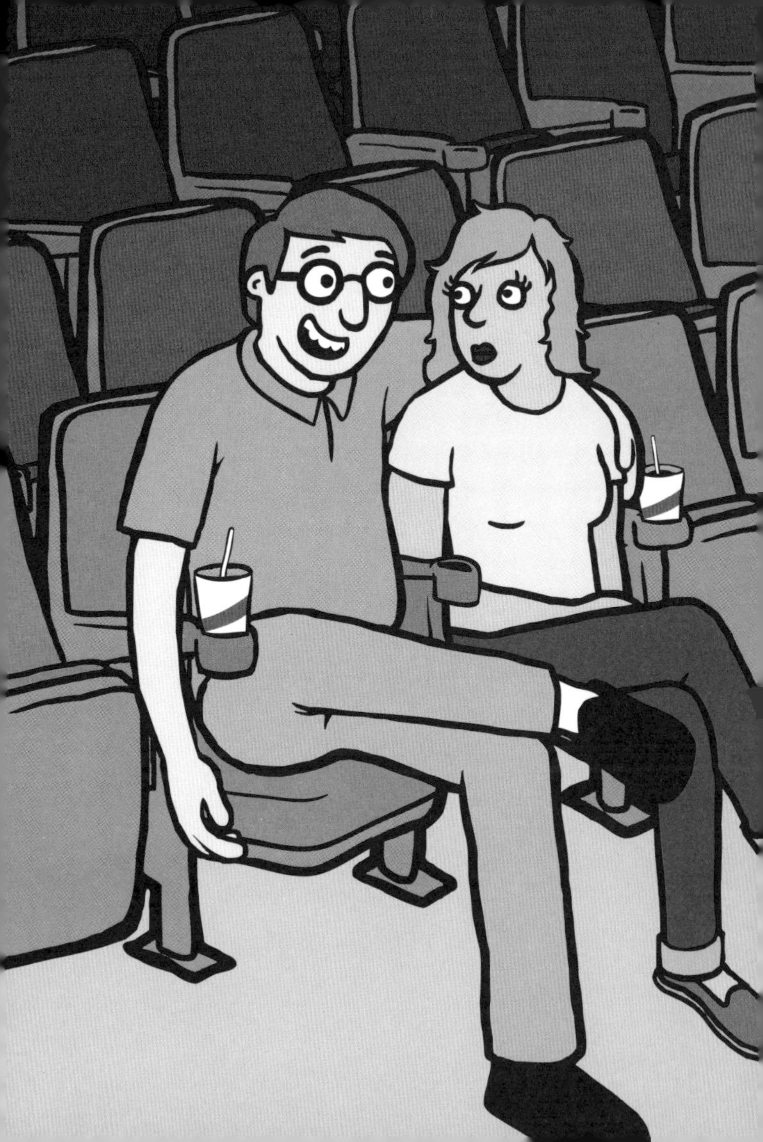

Something is seriously wrong with me.

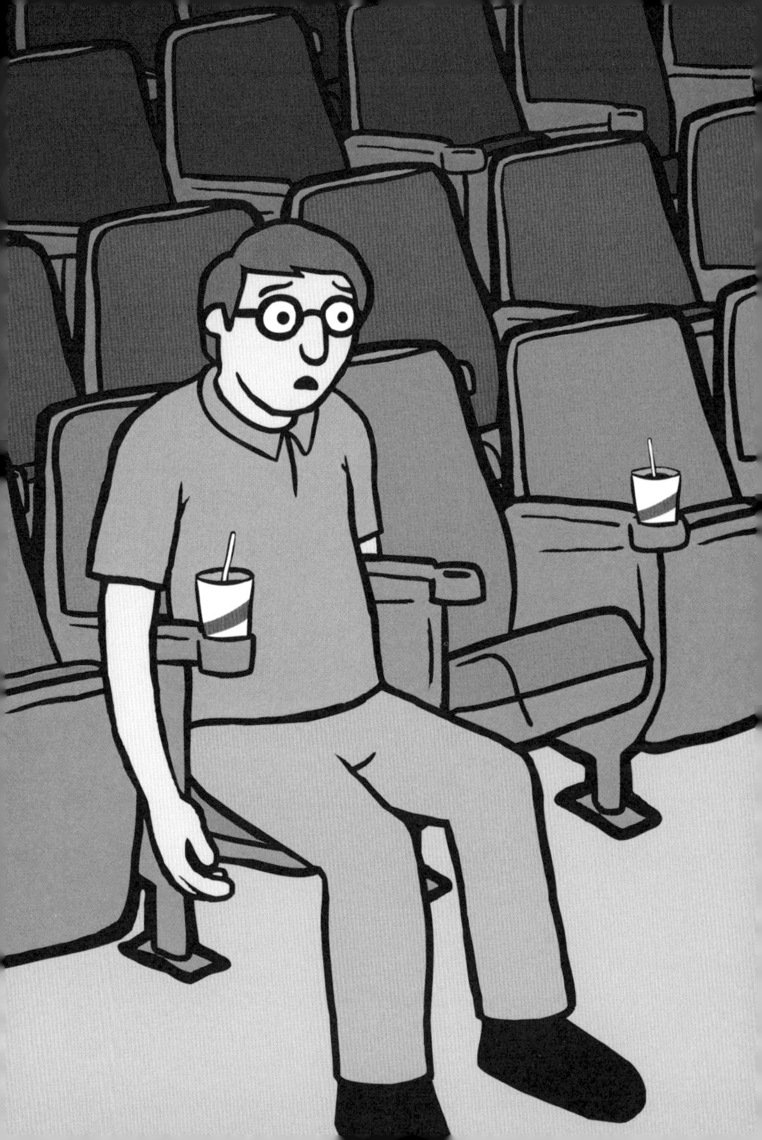

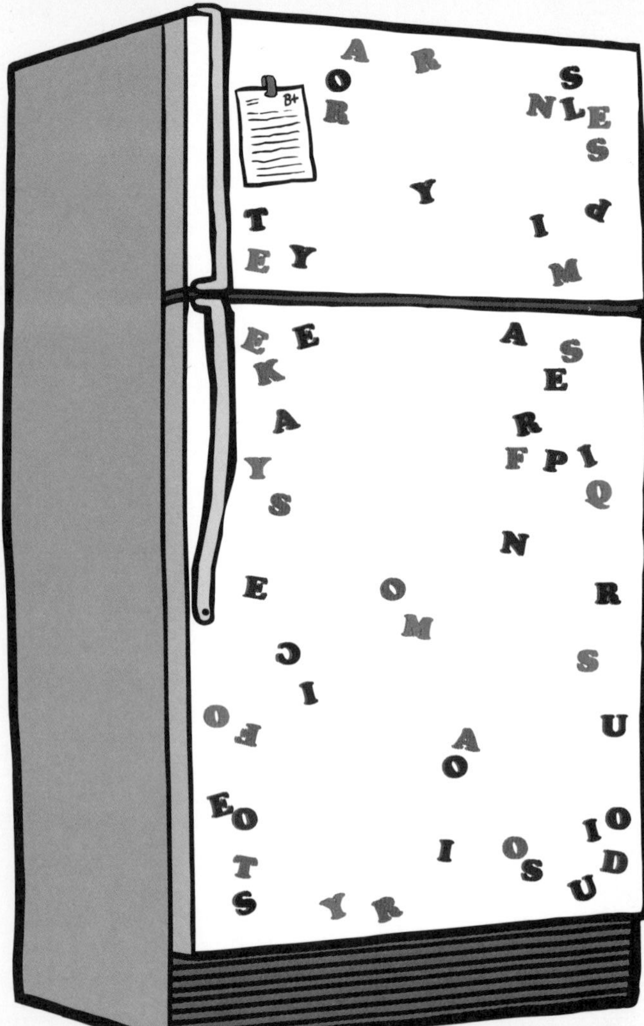
B+

Hello there, Mr. Refrigerator. Will you be my friend?

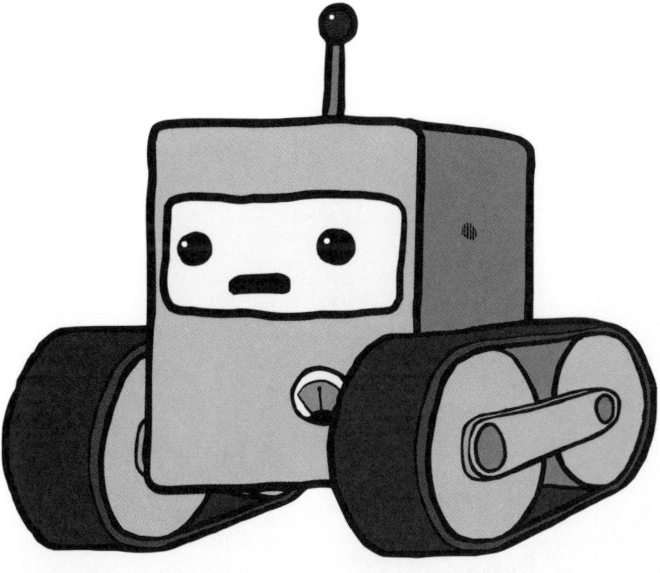

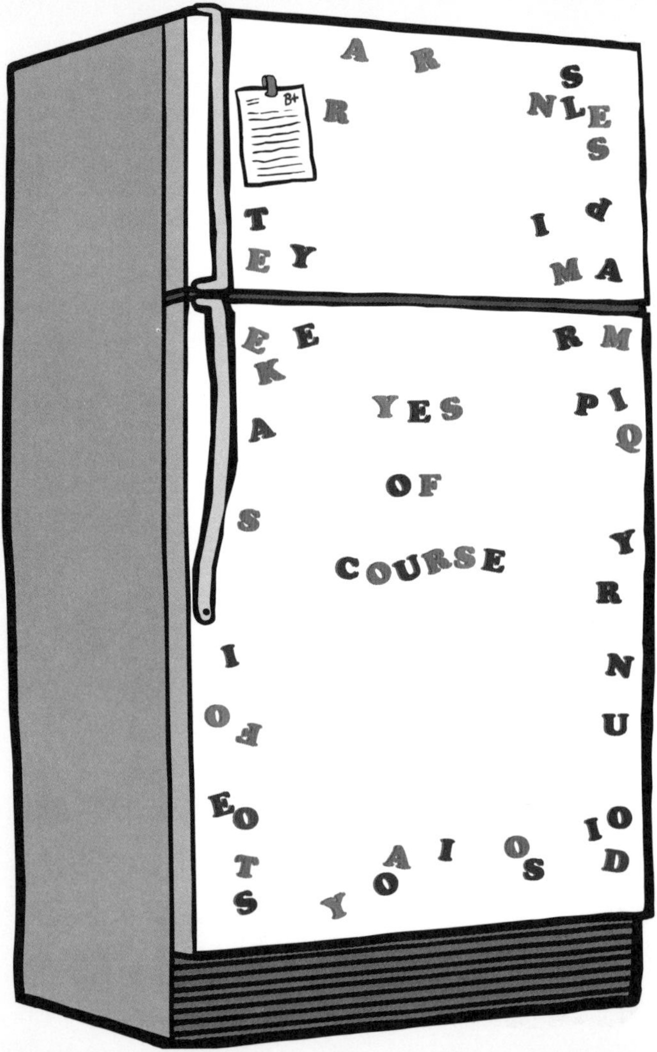
B+
YES
OF
COURSE

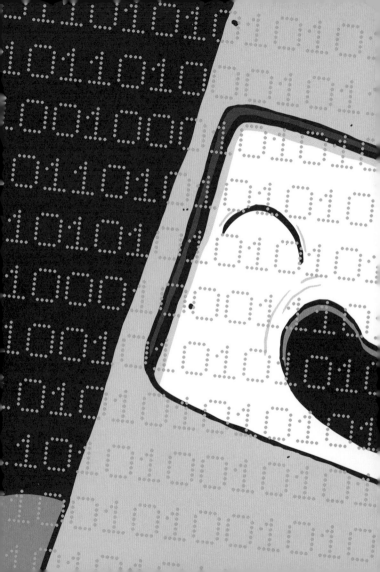

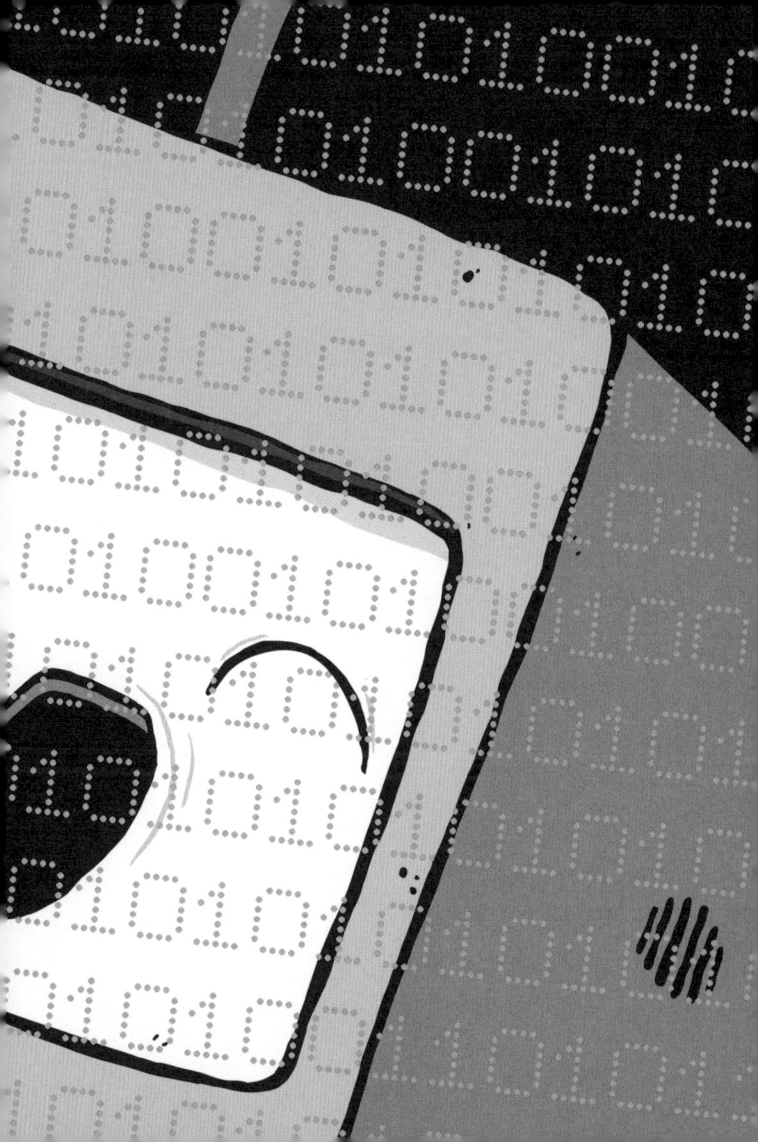

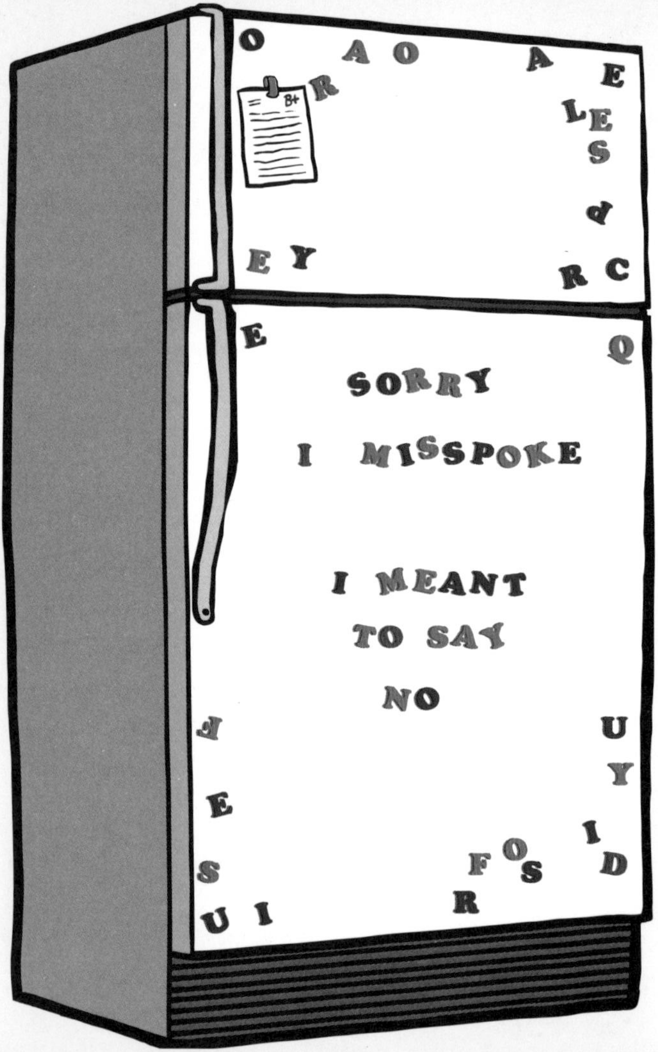
SORRY
I MISSPOKE
I MEANT
TO SAY
NO

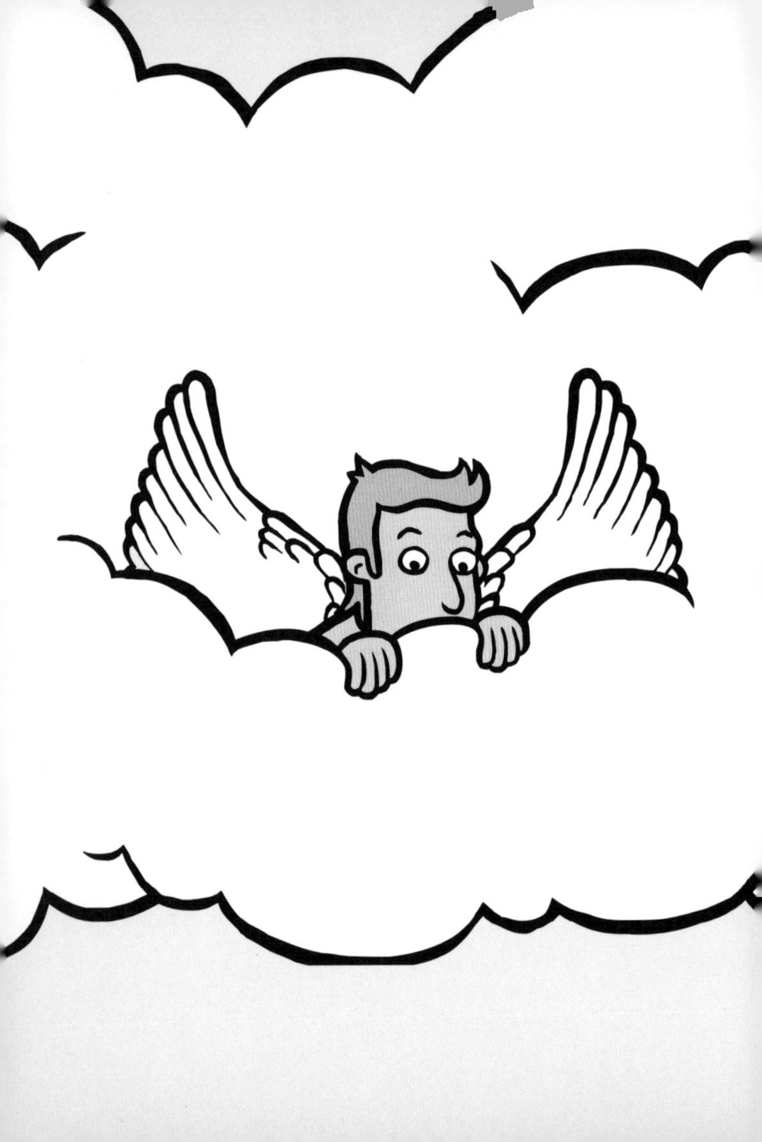

Yeah, girl. Work
that loofah.

I've really been trying to make friends, recently. It's just so hard to meet people these days.

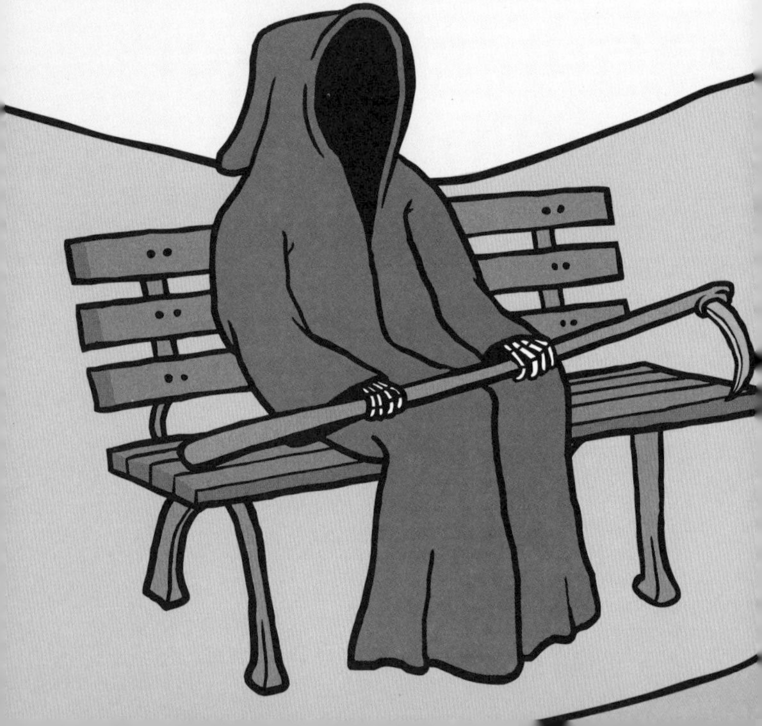

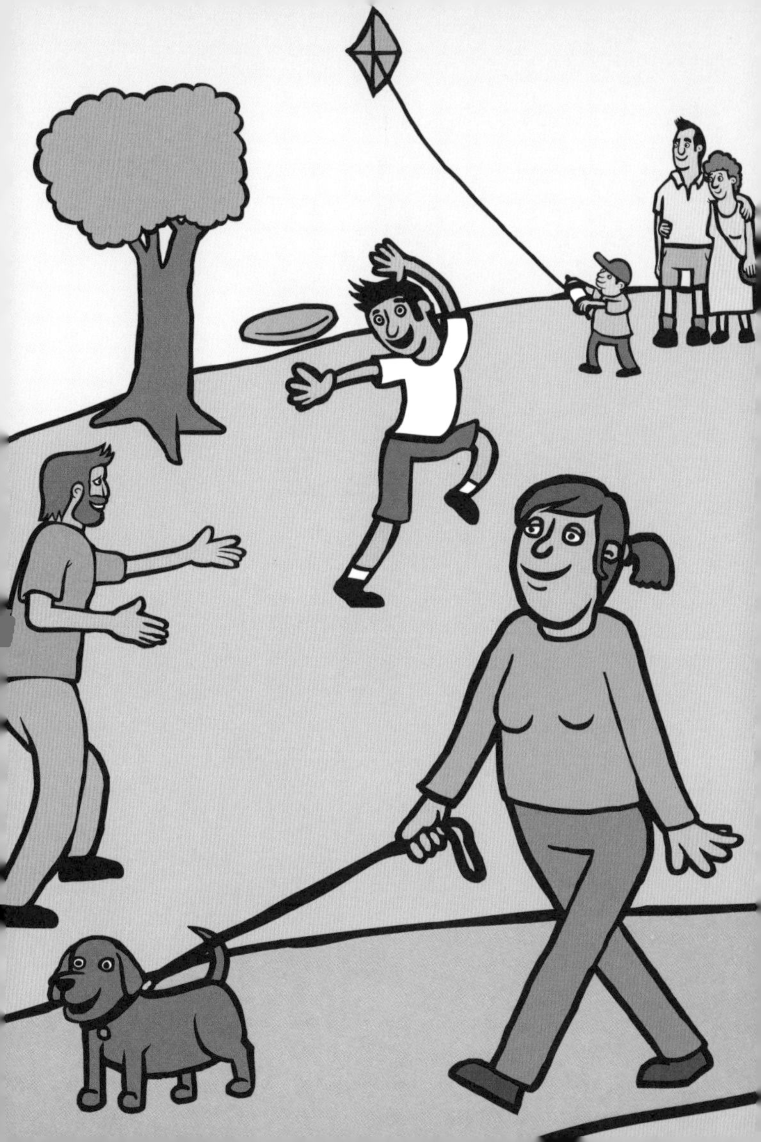

Whoops.

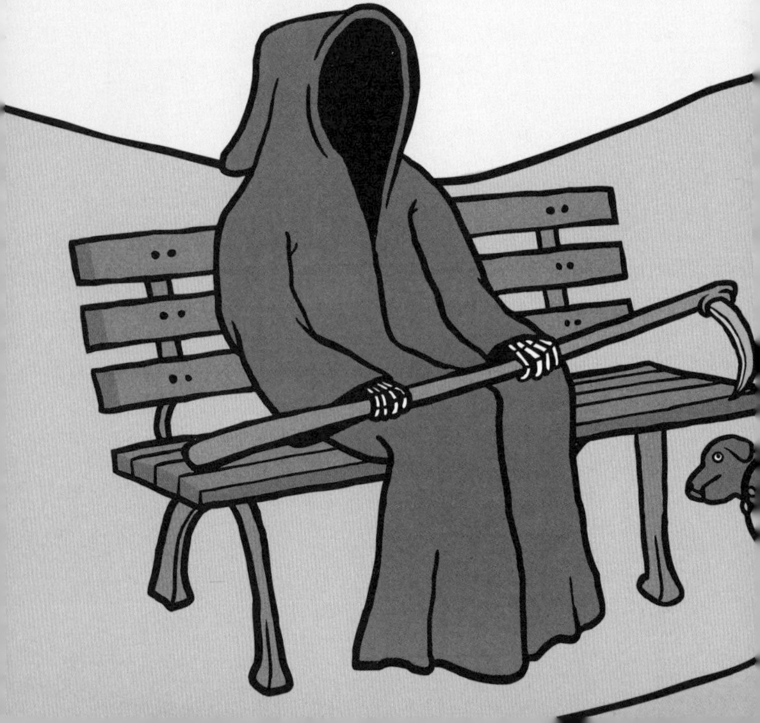

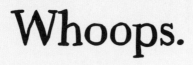

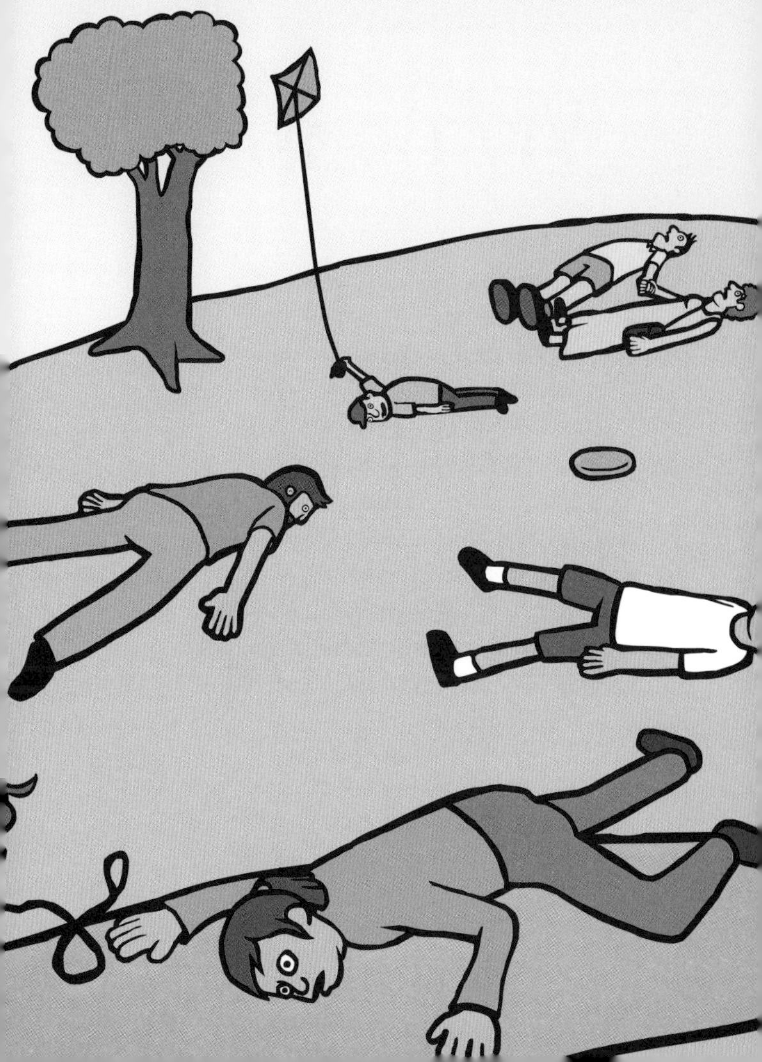

Acknowledgments

A thousand thanks to everyone at Chronicle Books, especially Steve Mockus, Emilie Sandoz, April Whitney, and Albee Dalbotten.

A huge thank you to Steven Malk, who makes a mean dinner playlist, among many other talents.

And our friends and families, including but not limited to: Allison Allbee, Joel Arquillos, Mac Barnett, Sarah-Violet Bliss, Jesse Brown, all the Cowans, Derek Fagerstrom & Lauren Smith, Zak Fishman, Zina Goodall, Walter Green, Emily Heller, Eli Horowitz, Deborah John, James Keary, Clare McNulty, Bill Monsen, Risa Monsen, Jeremy & Yvonne Otsu, Kate Parsons, Reddit, Gail Rubin, Patrick Shaffner, Ben Sinclair, Amanda Smith, Marielle Solan, Riley Soloner, Dan Weiss, and Lawrence Wilson. Thanks for being alive, guys.

About the Authors

Avery Monsen is an actor, artist, and writer who lives in New York. You should follow him on Twitter at @averymonsen.

Jory John is a writer, editor, and journalist who lives in California. On Twitter, he's @joryjohn. Why don't you follow him, too?

Together, they wrote *All My Friends Are Dead*, *I Feel Relatively Neutral About New York*, and *Pirate's Log: A Handbook for Aspiring Swashbucklers*. They also created the comic panel, *Open Letters*, which appears in weekly newspapers across the country. In their spare time, they make T-shirts at www.bigstonehead.net.

If you're on Facebook, and who isn't these days, you should come say hi at www.facebook.com /amfad.

My heart-valve has ruptured.

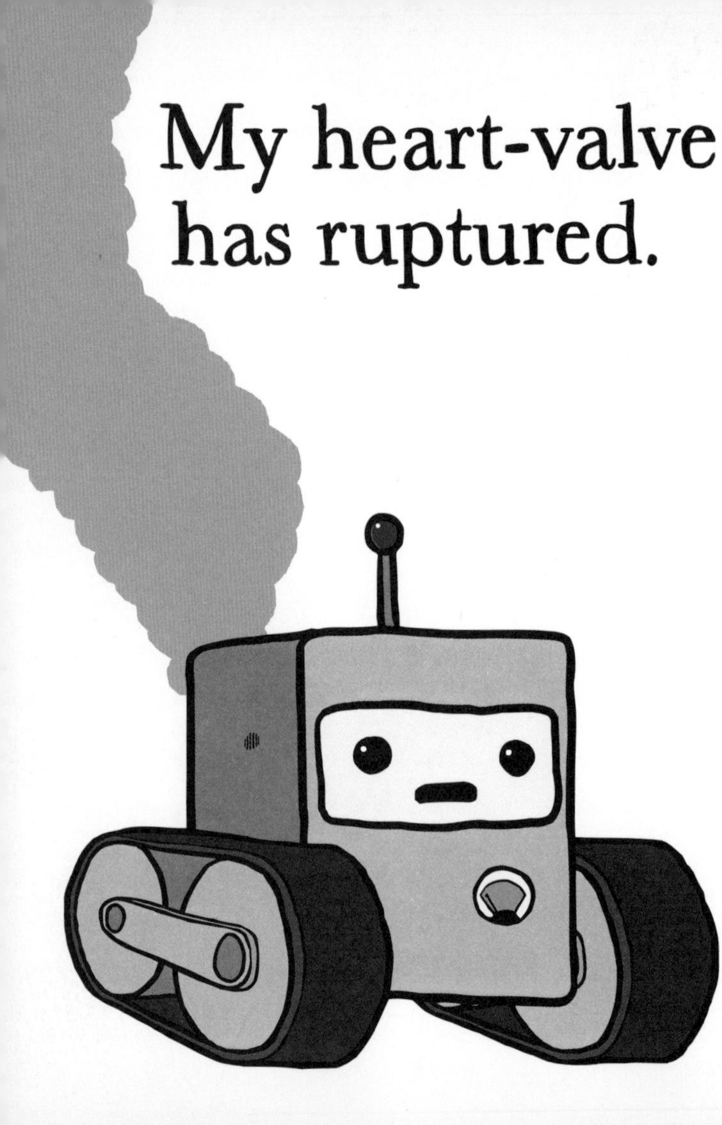